Staying the Course

HENRY M. JACKSON AND NATIONAL SECURITY

Staying the Course

Henry M. Jackson
and National Security

EDITED BY DOROTHY FOSDICK

UNIVERSITY OF WASHINGTON PRESS
Seattle and London

Library of Congress Cataloging-in-Publication Data

Staying the course.

1. Jackson, Henry M. (Henry Martin), 1912–   —
Views on national security.   2. United States—National
security.   3. United States—Foreign relations—
1945–   . I. Fosdick, Dorothy.
E840.8.J33S72   1987   327.73   87–2015
ISBN 0–295–96498–7 (cloth)
ISBN 0–295–96501–0 (paper)

To those who stayed the course with Scoop
and carry on in his tradition

Contents

Introduction

DOROTHY FOSDICK

Dorothy Fosdick is a member of the Board of Governors of the Henry M. Jackson Foundation and of the Visiting Committee of the Henry M. Jackson School of International Studies, University of Washington, Seattle.

She served with Senator Jackson as professional assistant and adviser on foreign and defense policy for twenty-eight years 1955–83 in a succession of positions including posts as professional staff member of the Subcommittee on National Policy Machinery 1959–62; Staff Director of the Subcommittee on National Security, Staffing and Operations 1962–65 and of the Subcommittee on National Security and International Operations 1965–73; Professional Staff Director of the Permanent Subcommittee on Investigations unit on national security matters 1973–81; and as Special Assistant to the Senator for National Security Affairs.

She came to the Senator's staff after ten years in the State Department (1942–53), with four years as member of the Policy Planning Staff, Office of the Secretary of State. Her books include *Common Sense and World Affairs* (1955). AB 1934 Smith College; PhD 1939 Columbia University.

In early January 1941, on a snowy night at Washington, D.C.'s Union Station, a 28-year-old lawyer from Everett, Washington stepped off the train. Some two months earlier Henry M. Jackson, former Prosecuting Attorney for Snohomish County, had been elected to Congress with the help of John Salter, a close boyhood friend and political ally, who was accompanying him on their first trip to Washington, D.C. The two young men picked up their bags, walked out into the night and called to a cabbie: "Where's the Capitol?" "Right over there, you dummies," said the cabbie, pointing to the Capitol dome just three blocks away.

Little did the cabbie know what lay ahead! That night marked the start of Jackson's forty-two years of continuous service in the Congress of the United States. He served from January 1941 until his death on September 1, 1983 at age 71. Jackson came to Congress the year Franklin D. Roosevelt began his third term—less than a year before Pearl Harbor. He would be re-elected to five more terms as Representative and to six consecutive terms as Senator from the State of Washington. His public service spanned fateful times: the age that saw the development of nuclear power; the age that saw technology shrink the world and expand its interdependence; and the age that saw the ideas and institutions of freedom and civility challenged around the world, and displaced in much of it by the totalitarian state.

Unlike so many political leaders who are on history's center stage for a few years, Jackson served the nation in the tenure of nine Presidents—Roosevelt, Truman, Eisenhower, Kennedy, Johnson, Nixon, Ford, Carter, and Reagan. In July 1983 Jackson's colleagues held a ceremony on the Senate floor as he cast his 11,000th Senate roll call vote.

In the early years of his congressional career, most observers assumed that when Henry Jackson made his full legislative mark it would be as champion of domestic causes and programs, especially those significant for that part of the country lying west of the Mississippi. This view turned out to be right insofar as it went—but it did not go far enough. By the close of his life, Jackson had compiled an extraordinary record of accomplishment on domestic matters in such areas as conservation, public recreation, water and power development, energy policy, and protection of the environment. One recalls his leadership in securing statehood for Alaska and Hawaii, settlement of the Outer Continental Shelf dispute, passage of legislation to create the National Wilderness System, establishment of the great Redwoods National Park in California and the North Cascades National Park in his home state, enactment of the Wild and Scenic Rivers Act, formation of the Youth Conservation Corps, passage of the Alaska Native Claims Settlement Act and the monumental Alaska National Interest Lands Conservation Act, enactment of the National Environmental Policy Act, and creation of the Strategic Petroleum Reserve.

But—what few foresaw in his earlier congressional years—Jackson also became a national leader in world affairs; a globally known authority and powerful participant in developing America's foreign and national security policies.

How did this come about? What was Jackson's role in foreign policy and national defense? How did he influence the course of events? And, finally, what is the Jackson legacy in national security affairs?

The essays in this volume focus on these questions and provide some of the answers. These essays do not, however, constitute a biography or a comprehensive account of the Senator's public career. They address only a part of the full Jackson story—albeit a central part for an understanding of American foreign and national security policy development over the past four decades.

The authors of these essays shared the privilege of Jackson's trusted association. They worked closely with him in one capacity or another in his House and Senate activities. As a result, they have direct knowledge and have drawn on personal recollection and anecdote to enliven their accounts. The range of their professional backgrounds and expertise suggests how the Senator reached out over the years to an unusually wide circle for help and advice.

JACKSON AND WORLD AFFAIRS

Jackson's early service in the Congress took place in the midst of World War II. He watched the Western democracies under desperate siege, and saw Norway, the homeland of his immigrant father and mother, under Hitler's heel. Rejecting isolationism as a tolerable option for America, he took his stand in the FDR tradition of accepting our responsibilities as a great world power. After Pearl Harbor, he served in the Army briefly as an enlisted man until recalled to the Congress by President Roosevelt.

In 1945, Jackson walked through the gates of Buchenwald a few days after the horror camp was liberated. That visit is usually interpreted as the experience that gave birth to his lasting concern with the fate of the Jewish people and the well-being of Israel. This is true, but it is not the whole truth. John Salter, his closest staff associate during those years, says the Buchenwald visit changed Jackson. All his work took on a new seriousness and a deep moral dimension. He had witnessed the total breakdown of law and civilization—of humanity itself—and he had taken his own private vow, "Never again."

During this early period, Jackson's approach to his duties was influenced and refined by his association and respect for Congressman Sam Rayburn and other key Southern Democrats. He listened and watched, learning the rules of the "club," its parliamentary procedures, and how leadership was and was not exercised. The Southern style in foreign affairs was congenial to him—a clear priority to safeguarding the nation and its democratic values, and a commitment to the principle that in national security matters, the "best politics" is "no politics."

The Democratic victory in the election of 1948 was for Jackson a milestone event. It enabled him to gain a seat on the Joint Congressional Committee on Atomic Energy, thereby giving him the chance to focus his energies on foreign policy and defense issues and to help shape the national response.

Sooner than most others, he came to realize how modern weaponry could endanger the peace if the Soviets outperformed the free nations, but also how a strong free world could help the cause of credible deterrence and peace. Believing that the Soviets might well achieve a hydrogen bomb before we did, he sided with those who argued we had no alternative but to go forward with a program of our own. He also had a leadership role in expanding the scale and scope of our overall nuclear weapons program, and later a similar role in trying to ensure that we did not lag in the development of key delivery systems, including the Polaris submarine and intercontinental ballistic missile, which he saw as crucial deterrents to Soviet aggression against the West and to nuclear blackmail.

Jackson was also ahead of most of his contemporaries in proposing efforts to place these weapons under agreed international control and to move toward mutual disarmament. In later years, he thoroughly enjoyed recalling to those who regarded him as an unreconstructed "hawk," his sponsorship of a House Resolution in 1950 and 1951 calling for speedy agreement upon effective and enforceable disarmament which would cover conventional armaments, biological and chemical agents and atomic and hydrogen bombs. Jackson refused, however, to support any arms control initiatives that would not, in his judgment, serve the security interests of the nation and the survival of free peoples. In the formulation of arms control policy and as a leader in the legislative consideration of treaties and agreements, the Senator defined his role, in the phrase, "to improve them." He became central to the arms control process—the chief Senate architect and advocate for more than two decades of mutual, balanced, verifiable arms reduction proposals that would reduce the level of forces in a way to enhance strategic stability. His persistence has borne fruit in the decision by both Washington and Moscow to focus on "reductions" in ongoing arms control negotiations.

For all his interest in world issues, Jackson never made a serious move to be on the Senate Foreign Relations Committee. Rather, he was able to pursue a broad range of foreign affairs related objectives through four other Senate Committees of which he was a member: the Armed Services Committee, the Government Operations Committee, the Joint Committee on Atomic Energy, and later, the Senate Select Committee on Intelligence. Another favorite forum for Jackson was the NATO Parliamentarians' Conference and its successor, the North Atlantic Assembly.

Jackson had no illusions that the United States could go it alone in the world. He shared in the Truman administration's effort to salvage Europe with the Marshall Plan and, in the face of an emerging Soviet threat, to bond the shattered West in the North Atlantic Treaty Organization. Convinced that the hopes of the world for future peace and freedom depended so largely on a strong, economically sound and confident Atlantic Community, he became the Senate's watchdog for the Atlantic Alliance—championing a steady American commitment to its stability and effectiveness. He was the acknowledged Senate leader of a bipartisan coalition which, year after year, supported budgets and programs to assure continuity of responsible American participation in NATO.

Jackson believed it was important for government to be staffed and organized to produce timely decisions and effective action. He maintained that the dangers and complexities of the postwar era required the executive branch and Congress to raise their standards of performance. Starting in 1959, he directed a careful congressional review of the policy-making mechanisms set up by the National Security Act of 1947. That inquiry—followed over the years by hearings, studies and reports on the role of the Secretary of State and the Ambassador, and the international negotiating process—had a significant impact on the administration of national security policy and operations and continues to influence the nation's affairs today.

Perhaps as much as any person in the Congress, Jackson saw the preservation and nurturing of human rights as a central obligation of the United States. In his view, nations, especially powerful ones, that deny the basic freedoms deprive themselves of an effective public opinion to control their conduct—a situation that not only leaves their citizens unprotected from lawlessness and oppression, but is a menace to international peace. Thus, human rights—commonly considered as humanitarian or at most political—were to him also strategically significant. As it turned out, Jackson became the intellectual and political leader of a whole generation in thinking about the problems and dilemmas in encouraging respect for human rights abroad and in mustering the political courage to take principled action. Of special note: the Senator conceived and championed the Jackson-Vanik amendment to the Trade Act of 1974, opening the way for hundreds of thousands of Jews, Christians and others to escape from Soviet and East European persecution and to find freedom in the West. The amendment is still the law of the land and is at the heart of ongoing bargaining with the Kremlin for freer emigration.

As a close observer of the Middle Eastern scene, Jackson early became a staunch friend of the democratic State of Israel. His interest in Israel began with his humanitarian concern for the Jewish victims of Nazi persecution and the new state that was created to receive them. But his continued support stemmed more directly from politico-strategic considerations—his commitment to the human values of democracy, and the need for reliable allies to help protect them. He considered Israel an indispensable Western asset, but he was also very much concerned about the poverty, rivalries and instabilities of the region. In 1972, for example, he visited Iran, Saudi Arabia and other Middle East states to consult with their leaders and enhance his understanding of the possibilities for overcoming regional differences. In 1978, he proposed a "Marshall Plan" for the Middle East based on a full partnership with the Israelis and Egyptians, aimed in time to benefit all those in the Arab world willing to live in peace. This proposal is still under discussion.

Given Jackson's world view, and his roots on the shore of the Pacific Northwest, it is not surprising that he kept his eye on the East Asian and Pacific area—especially on China, not only as a strategic reality but also as a great nation in its own right. Well before Henry Kissinger's secret July 1971 visit to China, the Senator joined those advocating an opening to China. By early 1969 he was a leading proponent of expanded American ties. During his last decade in the Senate, he mastered the intricacies of Sino-American issues, made four official trips to China, and exerted unusual influence on the course of U.S.-China policy.

Jackson's insistence on a strong Western deterrent was coupled with a belief in the value of an on-going American dialogue with the Soviet Union. Given the deep gulf on issues and the dangers of confusion and miscalculation, he considered it essential that the two super powers continuously, directly, and clearly exchange their respective views. To this end, for example, he sponsored efforts to explore with Moscow some of the less difficult and less complicated issues where a clear mutual interest might make early agreements feasible including means to reduce the fear of surprise attack, limitations on the spread of nuclear and chemical weapons to additional countries, and methods to prevent war by accident or failure of communication. In 1982, Jackson proposed the establishment of a special nuclear-risk reduction center or centers for continuing U.S.-Soviet dialogue to reduce the chances of war by accident, miscalculation or through terrorism. This initiative is under active negotiation in U.S.-USSR arms control talks.

During the last year of his life, Jackson became immersed in the growing problems in Mexico and in the rest of strategically important Central America. He concluded that achieving stable, democratic institutions in that area depended not only on American security assistance to assure an open future, but also on economic aid to help overcome the serious poverty and social inequities being exploited by the communists. To dampen a rancorous congressional debate and to work towards a bipartisan consensus, he proposed a Bipartisan Commission on Central America. The Commission had barely begun its work when the Senator died.

THE JACKSON STYLE

Early on, Jackson's older sister Gertrude had nicknamed him "Scoop" after a little boy in a comic strip who was very good at getting others to do what he wanted. Scoop liked his nickname—and he had an all-purpose nickname for those closest to him: "Leader." "What's our plan, Leader?" "How are we going to round up the votes we need, Leader?" It was a game that all of Scoop's colleagues, friends and troops understood. They knew who *their* leader was.

Like many who serve in the House and Senate, Jackson was able to attract highly competent people. He differed from many of his colleagues, however, in that he was also a great teacher for those who had the opportunity to work with him. The Jackson magnetism arose from: his knowledge of history and his ability to produce examples and analogies from man's prior experience that provided guidance for current issues; his practice of involving staff and advisers as equals in the process of policy development; his willingness to share his power with those who earned his trust; his candor in acknowledging when he didn't know the answer to a problem; his intellectual zest to enlarge his comprehension of the world; his critical, but open and youthful, capacity to take on new ideas and concepts; his inherent distrust for ideology and rigid philosophy as a source of answers to human problems; and finally, his fundamental respect for the process of dialogue and those who entered it honestly and used it intelligently.

Jackson was a skilled judge of people. The characteristics he looked for could not be papered over by advanced degrees, by expertise or by jargon. He was searching for elemental qualities he most valued—common sense, good judgment and integrity.

The Senator took great care in choosing the issues he became identified with. Was it one where his initiative or participation could make an important difference? Were the significant viewpoints receiving proper attention? Was it ripe for action, or was patience the wiser course?

Typically, Jackson steered toward results. What is the heart of the issue? What would untangle the problem and move things forward? Who could be most helpful? What bases should be touched to assure the required support? His speeches were very seldom given as ends in themselves—most were designed as part of a strategy to get something done.

Scoop had an instinct for the organization of consensus and action around a piece of legislation—a bill, an amendment, or a resolution. Coalition-builder par excellence, he lined up the help of Democrats and Republicans, one by one—on the Senate floor, in committee, in the cloakroom, in Capitol hideaways, on the Senate subway, in the Senate dining room, and, in the evening, in the steam room and swimming pool of the Senate gymnasium.

As much as any other politician in the 1970s and 1980s, Jackson was accessible to the news media. He set a record for Sunday news show appearances. He was available to editorial boards. For any reporter who wanted to do an in-depth substantive piece on matters of interest to Scoop, the door was open. But, they risked paying a price. He was not an entertainer. He might not deliver the quote they wanted. He resisted the facile analysis. He was part professor and part prosecutor. Jackson educated through the press and, at the same time, probed for information; the press, for Jackson, was both a tough critic on which to try new concepts and ideas, and usually, a good barometer of public attitudes.

The Senator was a popular 49-year-old bachelor when in January 1961 he met Helen Hardin of Albuquerque, New Mexico in, of all places, a Senate elevator. She was 29, the newly arrived receptionist in the office of Senator Clinton Anderson of New Mexico. They were married later that year. Helen Jackson proved to be the perfect partner for this incredibly dedicated and busy public servant. Scoop was very lucky in having Helen and their two children, Anna Marie and Peter Hardin, of whom he was inordinately proud.

The story is still told how the Senator interrupted his honeymoon in Hawaii to attend a Navy briefing at Pearl

Harbor on the Soviet submarine presence in the Pacific. Certainly, Scoop had his special ways. His family, friends and associates, even today, find wry—but fond—amusement in recollecting them: his complete lack of knowledge of most things "fashionable"; his extreme concern and care with a dollar; his persistent practice of diagnostic medicine; his notorious impatience as a back-seat driver; his compulsion to play mother hen to all of the children and young people he had an association with; his sometimes too earnest and monotone delivery of speeches when relying on a prepared text; his too easy accessibility to almost everybody; his personal fail-safe filing system— consisting of dozens of $9'' \times 12''$ brown manila envelopes piled all over his office—which he protected from every attempt at organization; his habit, when leaving his office on a trip, of sending everyone scurrying around in all directions, gathering memos for the "trip file," checking on flight plans, schedule times, and reminding them of necessary, last-minute phone calls.

Throughout his career, Scoop perceived and weighed his decisions on significant policy issues from a national and, where apt, an international point of view. This was a conscious ordering of priorities; a thought process he followed before considering the impact of a particular decision on his constituents, his party, or his own political aspirations.

He imposed on himself, and insisted that his staff observe, careful factual development and rigorous analysis of pending issues. If a matter was important to the core set of values and convictions he believed in as an individual and as a national Senator, then he spoke to and acted on those values. As a result, Jackson exercised an uncommon degree of independent judgment in taking positions that advanced the larger interests of the nation over the lesser interests which motivate so much congressional decision-making.

George Will wrote of Scoop's handling of the pressures in a democratic society in these words:

> Henry Jackson mastered the delicate balance of democracy, the art of being a servant to a vast public without being servile to any part of it. He was the finest public servant I have known.[1]

This is not to say that Scoop did not represent the economic and other concerns of his constituents effectively. His attention to his "home folks" and his ability, together with his colleague, Senator Warren G. Magnuson, to deliver, were legendary. The Jackson-Magnuson pipeline to the Pacific Northwest was a marvel: Federal hydroelectric projects on the Columbia River system, authorization of new reclamation projects, siting and funding of shipyards and military bases, low-cost electric power to attract basic industry, regional offices for most departments of government, and a host of other State and regional benefits.

THE NATIONAL LEADER

Throughout the latter half of Jackson's career in Congress, his conviction, independence and courage were most manifest on those difficult decisions in the 1960s and 1970s which determined the current course of this country's role in world affairs. These decisions dealt, for example, with the Vietnam War and its aftermath; detente; the Soviet "peace" offensive against Western Europe; human rights; the crude oil shortage and the economic crises of the mid-70s; Moscow's invasion and genocidal policies in Afghanistan; Soviet adventurism in Asia, Africa and Latin

America; the role of the intelligence community; strategic and conventional defense policy; the opening to China; and arms control negotiations. Jackson played a leading role in the debates on each of these issues, sometimes serving as the slow and steady fulcrum that moved policy in new directions; at other times, providing the force of persistent logic and rationality which deflected the flood of public and congressional emotion into institutional channels of reasoned debate and decision.

One result of filling this frequently vital role was that Jackson's views were often ahead of their time and, therefore, controversial; occasionally, they were consciously misrepresented, both in the media and by opponents.

Many in public life whose careers lend themselves to caricature are marked by fatal tendencies toward silliness, impulsiveness or meanness of spirit. Scoop clearly had none of these tendencies, yet, during this period, he was the subject of more than his share of "hard" political labeling and cartooning—Jackson the "hawk"; the "Senator from Boeing"; George Meany's "Senator for big labor." The raw and arresting nature of this form of distorted stereotyping is itself the product and reflection of the importance of the underlying issues and of Jackson's central part in those national debates.

Senator Ted Stevens of Alaska characterized Jackson's role and influence this way:

Scoop's contributions were, for a Senator, unprecedented. He determined the course of much of our nation's history in the 60s and 70s. Almost singlehanded, he turned back many of the emotionally supercharged movements for fundamental change that swept the country and the Congress during this era. Jackson refused to see the United States' traditional role in international affairs forfeited by Congressionally sanctioning national guilt, by turning inward, and by reversing our historic commitments.

I often wonder where the country might be today had we not had the benefit of his unswerving common sense, his voice of reason and his far-sighted leadership. Without Jackson's guidance, this would be a far different country than it is today. Many Presidents do not have a similar claim on the course and direction of this nation's history.[2]

Jackson's "inner compass" of core values and convictions kept him on a steady and predictable course of national purpose and national interest. Scoop was his own man. He had his own analysis of foreign policy and domestic matters. He was able to resist transient pressures of politics and the urgings of special interests and stay the course when emotion, fashionable sentiment and public outcry drove so many others to take cover.

In the words of Charles Krauthammer:

Jackson not only stood his ground, he never lost his equilibrium. He bestrode the center, while others sought refuge from the responsibilities of the Western alliance and the welfare state. He believed, with the Preamble to the Constitution, that the purpose of the Union was to provide both for the common defense and the general welfare.[3]

Scoop thus became a prominent and dependable landmark on the political scene. He represented reliable bedrock from which others could take bearings to find out where the country had been, where it was going, and why. Colleagues in the Senate went so far as to actually read and listen to his speeches and floor statements for the simple purpose of staking out their own position on complex and confusing national security matters. They did so confident on the basis of prior experience that Jackson's positions were carefully thought out, fully defensible, and not subject to change without good reason.

Because his views were steadfast, and because he could be counted on, Jackson developed over time a national and international following of more depth and reach than many Presidents. This same support encouraged his 1972 and 1976 campaigns for the Democratic Party's Presidential nomination. Amazingly, his following both at home and abroad increased after the two Presidential campaigns: Scoop's lack of success on the hustings invited informed comparisons with what might have been.

Presidents, Cabinet members, party leaders—and the officialdom of nations around the world—came to recognize that the Senator was a powerful personage on the national and international scene who could, if so moved, set the agenda for fundamental developments in world and domestic affairs.

Jackson respected and loved the Senate as an institution. He was a master in influencing Presidential policy by sending powerful signals from the Senate floor, in the form of statements and amendments that shaped and pushed administration policy in new directions. He looked for opportunities to write confidential letters which pointed the White House toward initiatives or compromises that would enable it to break log-jams in policy-making. However, when an administration failed to move in directions he thought prudent and necessary, he made his arguments, on the record, for publicly disengaging from the White House on policy grounds. Knowledgeable observers recognized the significance of such moves. Jackson consistently followed his legal training by building a careful and well-constructed case for his positions.

The posthumous description of Scoop by Senator Howard Baker of Tennessee is on the mark:

A man of majestic stature, of strength and conviction; a man who could stand on the Senate floor and express the conscience of the Congress and the country; a man who could change the course of debate and shape and form the policy of a great Nation; a man who was humble in the face of success and congratulations and who was courageous and determined in the face of criticism and dissent; a man who knew who he was and where he was going and where he wished to take the country . . .[4]

A SENSE OF HISTORY

The Senator's perception of priorities, values and direction was based upon and fed by his understanding of history. He had a long view of events and an appreciation for the frailty of the human condition. History fascinated him—with its insights into the roots of current issues, its disclosure of the heights and depths of human behavior, and its lessons on the fragility of peace, justice and personal freedom. Comprehending—and applying—the experience of history was in his mind the basis of "good judgment" in public affairs. "History," Scoop said, "is the great corrective for the distortions, exaggerations, errors, bombast, and verbal abuses of the present."[5]

Anna Marie Jackson remembers her father as the indefatigable "history teacher," helping on school assignments she had trouble with. Recalling one of his phone calls from New York after a busy day of speeches, she says he insisted on staying on the phone "until I understood the history of the New Deal backwards and forwards. That particular phone call took 2½ hours."[6]

Jackson was never reluctant to turn a congressional hearing into a history seminar. Aspiring young people seeking his advice on what to study were told: "Study history." When on an official trip abroad, he followed his own advice. He not only met with top leaders to explore policy concerns, but took time for an "on-the-spot" look into the history and culture of the nations visited. Throughout his official life, he drew on a group of historically oriented advisers whom he informally consulted—in person, by letter and by phone. Among the most trusted were Bernard Lewis, Professor of Near Eastern Studies, Princeton University, and Malcolm MacIntosh, Consultant on Soviet and East European Affairs for the British Cabinet Office. His treasured books were historical studies—a favorite being *Tsars, Mandarins, and Commissars; History of Chinese-Russian Relations* by Harry Schwarz (1964).

The Senator often drove home a point with a quotation reflecting historical experience; one he liked best was from the theologian Reinhold Niebuhr:

> There has never been a scheme of justice in history which did not have a balance of power at its foundation. If the democratic nations fail, their failure must be partly attributed to the faulty strategy of idealists who have too many illusions when they face realists who have too little conscience.[7]

Given Scoop's keen sense of history, contributors to this volume felt comfortable in undertaking to write about the aspects of his public service in which they shared first hand.

The authors are greatly indebted to many individuals who have helped them in the preparation of these essays. It is impossible to mention them all by name, but grateful appreciation should be expressed to three persons in particular.

William Van Ness, former chief counsel to the Senate Interior and Insular Affairs Committee during Jackson's tenure as Chairman, gave constant encouragement and his careful reading of the full manuscript provided many wise and helpful suggestions. Jane Hershman, supervisor of the Henry M. Jackson Papers Project at the University of Washington in Seattle, responded efficiently to the frequent requests for materials not easily available. Above all, Julia Cancio, longtime manager of Jackson's personal office, must be credited with bringing this book into being. She not only typed and watched over the manuscript, but her professional skills in research and editing were indispensable.

The Early Years

J. K. MANSFIELD

John Kenneth Mansfield was appointed by President Kennedy as the first Inspector General of Foreign Assistance in the Department of State serving from 1962–69. In 1978 President Carter appointed him the first Inspector General of the Department of Energy. Since 1981 he has been an industrial consultant.

After serving on the international faculty of Yale University, from 1950–56 he worked with Jackson as professional staff member of the Joint Congressional Committee on Atomic Energy—for two years while Jackson was Congressman and during the Senator's first four years in the Senate. Following the post of Assistant to the Director of the Nuclear Division of Combustion Engineering, Inc., he served from 1959–61 as Staff Director of the Subcommittee on National Policy Machinery, chaired by Senator Jackson. He subsequently assisted Jackson as a consultant on scientific and technical manpower to U.S. Delegations to the NATO Parliamentarians' Conferences and an adviser on weapons systems and arms control issues. BA Northwestern University; MA Yale University.

Scoop Jackson was in his fifth term as a Congressman when I met him in 1950, after forsaking the precincts of academe for a position on the staff of the Joint Congressional Committee on Atomic Energy, of which he was a member.

WHERE HE CAME FROM

The then 38-year-old Henry Martin (after Martin Luther) Jackson represented the District in which he had been born and raised—the State of Washington's Second—and Everett, its largest city, was his hometown.

Many of the people living in Everett were of Scandinavian descent and Jackson's mother and father were both Norwegian born. His ancestry, his boyhood home, and the place in which he grew up all influenced Scoop heavily.

Jackson embraced the values that his parents had brought with them from the old country to America. Life was not a lark; we were here on earth to do serious things. Hard work, frugality, self-reliance, honesty, steadiness, and stoicism in times of trouble were major virtues. Right and wrong were completely different things—not just varying shades of the same color.

Jackson also inherited much of his parents' politics. They were Democrats, of a persuasion reflecting what Norway's Labor Party had stood and worked for. From their perspective, there was nothing whatever radical about the Roosevelt revolution which many Americans viewed with dismay. The economic and social legislation under the New Deal was much like the laws that had been written in Norway decades earlier.

Scoop was proud of his ancestry. Throughout his life he would think about lessons to be drawn from the Norwegian experience for the governance of his own country.

Norway's experience under laws that cushioned people against the impact of economic calamities not of their own making, that safeguarded civil liberties, and that prevented the spoliation of Norway's magnificent endowment of nature reinforced Jackson's conviction that many of the domestic programs associated with the post-1932 Democratic Party could promote the well-being of his fellow Americans.

Norway's thralldom after Germany's legions invaded it in 1940 underscored his conviction that insuring the survival and independence of America was the first and highest responsibility of any administration. Of what avail to Norway's people was all its clean air and pure water, he would frequently ask, once Hitler's troops had set foot on Norwegian soil?

The Everett, Washington in which Scoop was raised was a workingman's town—he was himself the son of a mason. But programs which have been taken for granted for decades—social security, unemployment insurance, workmen's compensation and the like—were in Jackson's early years programs seriously at issue; programs that were still being debated and battled for.

The lumber and paper mills around which Everett's economy was built were at the time serious polluters of the air and water. "A very nice place with great people, but it smelled awful," a close Jackson associate said.

So the economic and social programs he would vote for
in the Congress, and the great environmental protection
programs he did so much to help create, were for him not
things that were just good in the abstract. The need for
these programs was deeply rooted in his own experience.

Jackson's Everett was a small Western town. Its citizens
were for the most part open, neighborly, frank and unpre-
tentious. Office holders who forgot where they came from
and began to put on lordly airs quickly found themselves
ex-office holders. Surely it says something important
about Henry Jackson that his hometown's voters gave him
resounding majorities in every one of his congressional
races—twelve straight times.

Although he would come to spend forty-two years in the
nation's capital—twelve as a Congressman and thirty as a
Senator—spiritually he never left Everett. And he never
doubted that he would return and spend his remaining
days there when his career of public service had ended.

WHERE HE WAS GOING

Scoop had been in the House of Representatives for almost a decade when I met him.

In the Congress a member's committee assignments
largely determine the issues on which he spends his time.
In Jackson's case, the committees on which he sat during
his first eight years in the House (most importantly Mer-
chant Marine and Fisheries, Indian Affairs, Small Business, and briefly, Appropriations) were not primarily concerned with national security issues. Of course, like all
Representatives, Scoop voted on matters relating to national security, but most of his legislative energies were
focused on domestic questions.

But this changed in 1949 when, following Harry Truman's upset victory and the recapture of the House by the Democrats, Scoop was assigned a seat on the Joint Congressional Committee on Atomic Energy. Thereby, he obtained an unusual opportunity and responsibility both to learn about critical national security issues and to do something about them.

The Joint Committee was the congressional watchdog of the national atomic energy program. The Atomic Energy Commission, the executive branch agency that ran the program, was required by law to keep the committee "fully and currently informed" about its activities. As a result, Committee members possessed top secret information of the highest sensitivity to which other members of the Congress were not privy. They were kept abreast both of what the nation was doing in atomic weaponry and of what the intelligence community thought the Soviet Union was doing. Because the Committee members knew things that other members of the Congress did not know, their views were carefully heeded by their colleagues.

In the immediate post-World War II years, Western Europe was economically prostrate, the Marshall Plan and NATO were still just gleams in the State Department planners' eyes, and Soviet conventional armed forces dwarfed those of the United States and countries friendly with it. The grand strategy we adopted for keeping the peace was posited on answering brawn power with brain power and quantity with quality—on offsetting Soviet superiority in conventional weapons and numbers of troops with advanced weapons that were technologically and militarily superior to the armaments in Soviet arsenals. And the most important element by far in this strategy was the deterrent power of the atomic weapons of which the United States was then the sole possessor.

The issues which Scoop would now address as a new member of the Joint Committee on Atomic Energy therefore went to the very heart of our efforts to contain Soviet power.

Committee membership would also give him major insights into the very tough problems faced in trying to work out acceptable international agreements for limiting and reducing nuclear arms. It had been relatively easy to verify compliance with the agreements signed in the early 1920s to place limits on the capital ships in the navies of the great powers. A battleship was not easy to hide. In contrast, how could nations assure compliance with agreements for reducing numbers of nuclear bombs or warheads whose lethality derived from components small enough to be contained in a suitcase?

Just months after Scoop came on the Joint Committee, the Soviet Union broke America's atomic monopoly by exploding its first A-bomb. It did so years sooner than most experts had expected it would. In fact, the then head of our own atomic program believed that the Soviet Union might *never* be able to build an A-bomb.

A high-level governmental debate followed over whether a part of our national response to the Soviet's stunning achievement should be an effort to build a hydrogen bomb—a thermonuclear bomb—a weapon that would derive its destructive force from the fusing, rather than from the splitting, or fissioning, of atoms. Nobody knew if such a weapon could be built. But if it could be, an H-bomb might dwarf the power of the fission-type Hiroshima and

Nagasaki A-bombs in the same way that they had dwarfed the power of conventional bombs.

A majority of the Commissioners of the Atomic Energy Commission argued against an immediate attempt to develop an H-bomb. So did the Commission's powerful General Advisory Committee. Meanwhile, Scoop had been named to a Special Subcommittee charged with helping the Joint Committee members arrive at a position on this issue.

The report summarizing the views of those opposed to an immediate attempt to build a hydrogen weapon advanced many arguments. Maybe an H-bomb could not be built. And if it could be built, maybe it couldn't be delivered. And if it could be delivered, maybe there weren't any targets big enough for such a weapon. And if there were such targets, maybe fission bombs would do the job just as well. And if we refrained from trying to build an H-bomb, maybe the Soviets would also refrain. And so forth.

Jackson saw the situation differently. The odds appeared to him to be at least 50-50 that such a weapon could be built. It was inconceivable to him that our failing to go forward with a development program would cause the Kremlin not to go forward. If we tried to build an H-bomb and failed, we might spend some hundreds of millions of dollars for which we got nothing tangible in return. But if the H-bomb proved to be feasible, and the Soviets built it while we had not, the cost to the United States in terms of lessened influence and diminished security would be immensely greater. So Scoop concluded that we had no alternative but to see whether a thermonuclear weapon was feasible. (By way of historical footnote: The issue of whether developmental forbearance on our part would elicit similar restraint from the Soviet Union was in truth a non-issue. While we had been debating, they had been working. Their own successful H-bomb program had been put on an all-out basis immediately after the test of their first A-bomb.)

Scoop strongly believed that a major effort to determine whether a thermonuclear weapon could be built must be accompanied by a parallel and equally major effort to see whether an agreement could be reached with the Soviet Union that would not only halt an H-bomb race but that would also produce arms cuts in other weapons categories.

Indeed, the first matter on which I assisted Scoop had to do with reducing nuclear weapons. This was a House Resolution he introduced in 1950 calling upon our government to invite all other governments—including the Soviet Union—to join with the United States, not only in across-the-board arms cuts, but also in using a substantial portion of the money that would thereby be saved on programs for helping raise standards of living in the poorer nations, and, in addition, urging that a session of the General Assembly of the United Nations be devoted to the single purpose of speeding progress on arms cuts accords. Again in 1951, and yet again in 1953, he introduced similar Resolutions.[1]

There were, however, no signs that Moscow was interested in serious arms control discussions. On the contrary, signs abounded that the Soviet Union was intent on retaining its superiority in conventional weapons, while, at the same time, increasing its lead in high technology areas where it was then ahead (as in being the first to hurtle a satellite into space) and on catching up with and, ultimately, surpassing the U.S. in areas where it then lagged.

Had the Jackson approach to the H-bomb question not prevailed, we would almost certainly have found ourselves in a position where the Soviet Union had thermonuclear weapons and we did not. Scoop did his best to help insure that we would not be outstripped by Moscow in other critical races for discovery then underway or in prospect. The influence he could bring to bear in this regard was to be increased by committee assignments that gave him a place on the Senate Armed Services Committee after he left the House in 1953. As a Senator he also served on the Joint Committee and became Chairman of a newly created Military Applications Subcommittee. The issues on which Jackson worked included the following:

Expanded production of fissionable materials. Scoop was remarkably prescient in anticipating how Soviet weapons stockpiles would grow if the two nuclear superpowers failed to arrive at accords on arms limitations. Absent such agreements, he foresaw, Moscow would come to possess thousands of nuclear weapons. If we were not to fall behind the Soviet Union in weapons output, Jackson saw a need for big stepups in the production of uranium-235 and plutonium—the fissionable materials required for the manufacture of both A-bombs and H-bombs. His urgings toward this end had much to do with the expansion program voted by the Congress in 1952.

The fight to save Admiral Rickover. The fact that the United States led in developing nuclear power for propelling submarines and naval surface ships was due in large part to the managerial and technical genius of the controversial Hyman Rickover, the father of the nuclear navy. Jackson was the most influential Senator in the successful battle waged in 1953 to save Rickover his job in the face of efforts by the Navy to deny him the promotion needed to keep him from forced retirement.

Ground Launched Ballistic Missiles. To insure that we would not trail Moscow in developing land-based ballistic missiles of both theater and intercontinental range, Jackson's Subcommittee held in-depth closed hearings on ways of accelerating our development program. Its recommendations were set forth in a top secret memorandum that was sent to the White House on June 30, 1955.[2] This report was directly responsible for President Eisenhower's receiving his first comprehensive briefing on the state of our ballistic missile effort.

Submarine Launched Ballistic Missiles. Sooner than most others, Jackson foresaw the great contribution that missiles launched from submarines, with their near invulnerability to a pre-emptive strike, could make to deterrence and to stability in the strategic balance. In 1956, a Jackson-appointed advisory group of distinguished experts on underseas warfare developed recommendations to insure that our ballistic missile submarine fleet would be adequate in size and in service on time.

The NATO Science Program. As Scoop saw it, it was imperative that the U.S. and its allies develop the kind of technological base that was needed to produce required innovations at a satisfactory pace. A Jackson-chaired committee of the Parliamentarians' Conference of the North Atlantic Treaty Organization persuaded the member governments to establish in 1958 a successful NATO program to help produce more and better scientists and engineers.

Jackson never believed, either in his early years in Congress or later, that American military strength would by itself suffice to keep the peace. Our armed forces, as he saw it, no matter how well trained or equipped, could never substitute for a wise diplomacy, for allies willing and able to share with us the responsibilities of peace-making, and for domestic economic and social programs aimed at creating a United States in which justice was so dispensed, economic opportunities so created, adversities not of one's own doing so mitigated, and individual liberties so protected that its citizens would be ready and proud to do whatever was needed to assure the survival of their country.

Yet, if adequate military strength alone was not adequate for national survival and keeping the peace, Scoop believed it was most surely a necessary condition precedent. How, he wondered, could anybody think otherwise after 1940's fateful spring.

Henry Jackson never believed, then or later, that building weapons could substitute for trying to control or reduce armaments. By the time I met him, he had already done much reading and talking about past attempts to arrive at arms cuts accords, and much pondering about what could be learned from these efforts. The conclusions he reached would stand the test of time.

For starters, he found himself out of step both with those who thought that just about any arms control agreement was bad, and those who thought any agreement was good. In his eyes, "Are you for arms control agreements?" was the wrong question. Instead, he believed, "What kind of agreements will make the world a safer place?" was the right question. In Jackson's view, agreements that would prevent the replacement of vulnerable or accident-prone weapons with more survivable or more reliable weapons would do the cause of peace a disservice, while agreements encouraging such replacements could make the world a less dangerous place.

Moreover, Jackson thought it completely reasonable for both the United States and the Soviet Union to insist that any weapons limitations or reductions agreed upon be verifiable, mutual and equitable. Jackson hoped (and worked to help assure) that the U.S. would not sign agreements compliance with which we could not confirm or pacts that tilted the strategic balance against U.S. interests.

In 1962 I left Capitol Hill, but I remained on call to Scoop and continued to assist him in consultative capacities. The first thing I had worked on with him were arms control matters—how to speed progress towards arms cut accords. The last thing on which I tried to help him also had to do with arms control—how best to guard against the danger of a nuclear war breaking out which neither side had either planned or wanted; a war that might be triggered as a result of an accident or miscalculation.

More and more the Senator had come to think it vital that Washington and Moscow stay in touch with each other when developments occurred that threatened the peace. Jackson was struck with the contrasting lessons that the outbreak of World War I and the Cuban missile crisis of 1962 offered in this regard. In the first case, Europe's statesmen failed to keep talking and consulting with each other; as a result, millions then died in a war none of the great powers had really wanted. In the second, Soviet and American leaders did keep talking with each other, and war was averted.

In 1982, Jackson became part of a small but influential group of Senators, including Senator Sam Nunn and Senator John Warner, who urged the establishment of what came to be called risk reduction centers.[3] These centers would stay in operation around the clock every day of the year, with Soviet and American representatives consulting face-to-face over conference tables when events occurred that could trigger an unwanted nuclear war, and reporting back to their governments information on and assessments of the position of the other side. This proposal is now under active negotiation with the Soviet Union.

WHAT HE WAS LIKE

The predominant impression that Scoop gave was one of a feet-planted-firmly-on-the-ground kind of stability and solidity. "A good man to have around in a hurricane," a friend said once of him.

His character mirrored the way he looked. Perhaps the ancient Romans had the best word for it—*gravitas,* in the sense of substance, serenity, steadiness, and seriousness of aim and of conduct. (In Jackson's lexicon, few words were more pejorative than "lightweight.") This was no dilettante, no dabbler, no stroller through the fields, plucking a flower here and a flower there.

One of the first things that struck me about Scoop was that quite early on—in important instances, before he came to the Capitol—he seemed to have arrived at some fundamental judgments about what the world was like, on what wanted changing and what did not, and on how best to preserve what was good and to change what was bad. Some of these judgments were ethical—for example, that the certain inalienable rights talked about in the Declaration of Independence were rights that belonged not just to Americans but to people everywhere. Others had to do with practicalities—for example, speeches and press releases were no substitute for working with others in trying to get things done. And once arrived at, these judgments or principles proved to be enduring ones that provided him, so to speak, with navigational aids for determining where events were moving and how he should place himself in relation to them.

So if one saw people in terms of sociologist David Riesman's "other-directed" and "inner-directed" character type groupings—radar-type people who think and act mainly in response to their perceptions of how other people are thinking and acting, as against gyroscope-type people who think and act largely in response to direction finders located deep within their own psyches—Jackson was clearly much closer to being "inner-" than "other-directed."

In the case of many people who remain on the national scene for as long as Scoop did, their personalities or their views or both change drastically over time. Keynsians in earlier years, for instance, may end up as supply-siders. Interventionists when they step on the public stage may become isolationists by the time the final curtain descends.

Not so with Henry Jackson. There was about Scoop a great constancy in terms of how he saw himself and the world. Where fundamental principles were concerned, the 71-year-old Senator Jackson who was feted by China's rulers in Beijing's Great Hall the week before he was struck down was the true successor to the 28-year-old Congressman Jackson who had to be told how to get from Union Station to the Capitol.

In others, such constancy might bring with it a rigidity of outlook. Scoop, however, was not merely receptive to, he was also constantly searching for, fresh departures in policy and new ways of dealing with issues. The man-on-the-moon program and the Jackson-Vanik amendment are two cases in point. President Kennedy's bold proposal to

land men on the moon within a decade traced back directly to a Jackson-drafted memorandum to the then President-elect urging him to declare this to be a national goal.
As for Jackson-Vanik, nobody had previously tried to do
what was accomplished through the amendment—using
United States trade policy as a carrot and stick to increase
the numbers of political dissidents, minorities and others
that the Soviet Union and other nonmarket economy
countries would allow to emigrate.

For those interested in how people in high office arrive
at the positions they do, Scoop was a fascinating study.
Like Marshal Foch with his constant *"De quoi s'agit-il?,"*
what he wanted to know when addressing some new national security question was, "What's it all about—what's it
really all about?"

The way he approached such issues must have been
what Justice Holmes had in mind in the superb passage in
his writings that says, "At this time we need education in
the obvious more than investigation of the obscure." In
grappling with an issue, Jackson did not allow himself to
become so preoccupied with secondary and tertiary considerations and minutiae as to lose sight of what was central and primary.

Scoop was extraordinary in getting to the heart of the
matter. In almost four decades of working for and observ-
ing public figures, many of them immensely talented, I
have never seen Henry Jackson's superior in this respect.

He was completely unhurried in making sure that he knew
what something was really all about. A case in point is the
Jackson-chaired bipartisan study conducted by his Subcommittee on National Policy Machinery from 1959 to 1961.
Twenty-five years later this study is still the benchmark re-

view against which similar examinations are measured. The Subcommittee staff, of which I was named director, spent almost six months in sending interrogatories to and interviewing scores of present and past officials and scholars in the field (with Jackson himself seeing most of those being consulted) before a single hearing was scheduled.

However, once Jackson was convinced that he understood an issue in its full roundness and depth, decisions came easily and with dispatch. There was no looking back, no rehashing, no agonizing reappraisals.

There was also a great coherence about his outlook. He saw problems not in isolation but against a perspective that became ever more global. Hence his views on one issue dovetailed with his views on others. Things fitted together.

In addition, for Jackson the past was most decidedly prologue. Because he knew about such things as past ambitions of expansionist powers and the successes and failures met in efforts to contain them, earlier twentieth century attempts to reach disarmament accords, and czarist as well as Soviet history, major happenings on the international scene rarely took him by surprise. He had warned for years, for example, of the danger of the Soviets occupying Afghanistan.

Like Harry Truman, he almost never encountered an issue on which he did not think history had something useful to say about how to deal with it. He therefore found it much easier to make decisions than did those who saw policy alternatives posed as *de novo* choices with no historical precedents.

The late Senator Carl Hayden (whose record for length of congressional service Scoop was fast approaching) once commented that members of the Congress could be sepa-

rated into showhorses and workhorses. Jackson belonged
unmistakably in the workhorse corral.

He was also a joy to work for. He looked for, he recognized, he appreciated, he gave credit for and praised staff
work of excellence.

In the Jackson world, blurred lines separated work from
play. The leader and his troops worked together and so-
cialized together. There was a period of Sunday morning
playground pick-up softball games in Georgetown in
which Senators Jack Kennedy and Mike Mansfield were
among the players. Although respectable enough, Scoop's
performance on the diamond would not have caused a
diMaggio to look to his laurels. But in the occasional post-
game contests to see who could spit watermelon seeds
farthest, Scoop displayed world-class talents.

With the Norwegian in Jackson came frugality. "I'm
tighter than the paper on that wall," he would proudly but
not wholly accurately proclaim. He had very few material
wants, and at the time I met him just about all of his
worldly possessions could be packed into two trunks that
kept crossing the continent, going to Washington when
the Congress convened and returning to Everett when it
adjourned. His automobile buying habits were not of the
kind that made dealers rich. His all-time favorite car was a
'61 Chevrolet that he inherited from his mother-in-law in
1966 and drove until 1982. It is a considerable understate-
ment to say that the manner in which Scoop drove this
noble vehicle was not fully worthy of the fidelity with
which it had served him. Indeed, office wags said they
should be entitled to hazardous duty pay for time spent
riding as passengers.

But where his conduct toward others was concerned, his
generosity was what stood out. Thus when he and his

Senatorial colleagues were required by law in 1978 to make public their income tax returns, it became widely known that since his election to the Senate in 1952 all of his not inconsiderable honoraria from speaking engagements had gone to people in need. The greater part went to a fund which Scoop had established in 1969 to help students in the Everett school district, especially those seeking scholarship aid. This fund was in memory of his sister, Gertrude, who was a third grade Everett teacher for over 40 years. And in a vocation where time was often a more precious commodity than money, Jackson was downright profligate in extending personal counsel and help to staff members, colleagues and friends.

Among the fringe benefits of working for Scoop was a lifetime guarantee of help from a job counseling and placement service of which he was both the chief executive officer and only employee. He went to great lengths to help present and past staffers in this regard. I recall, for example, coming upon Scoop alone in an office suite in a deserted Russell Senate Office Building on a gray November weekend shortly after the 1980 elections had stripped control of the Senate from the Democrats. Strewn on the floor around him were the resumes of Committee staffers who would be losing their jobs come January and on whose behalf he would be making dozens of phone calls to help them find work.

Health and finances were two of the subjects on which Scoop did not wait to be asked before giving advice to the staff.

A physical fitness buff, he could not resist summoning back to the paths of righteousness those who had strayed from them. Eat less, party less and exercise more—he would urge in my case. I would charge in turn that his idea of high living was an extra dollop of cottage cheese on the fruit salad that was his unvarying lunchtime fare. (The truth was somewhat different. Although he would always say, "Heavens, no," if asked in the Senate restaurant whether he would take dessert, he would urge upon staff members at the table desserts of outrageous richness and then proceed to cadge samplings shamelessly.)

In the management of his personal finances, Jackson was meticulous in avoiding any investments that could conceivably create the appearance of a conflict of interest. He was fond of pointing out that even buying United States savings bonds was not without problems in this regard, since members of the Congress voted on questions affecting interest rates and therefore the value of bonds.

However, he was an avid student of financial matters. He kept abreast of Wall Street happenings, he followed the market's ups and downs on a daily basis, and he gave much thought to hypothetical investment strategies.

If Jackson felt constrained by his public office from putting his investment acumen fully to the test in his own affairs, he saw no need to deny himself the vicarious pleasure of trying to help staff members along the road to solvency. He participated with gusto in their house buying and selling decisions, and he was never so busy that he could not take time out to offer them stock market advice.

Scoop delighted in sharing with his staff, and with its more junior members, things he believed he had learned during the practice of his calling. "Always keep your word" was a favorite piece of advice. One of the first things he had found out as a Congressman was that the legislative process simply does not function if people fail to do what they say they will do—by reneging, for example, on promises to support one bill, and to oppose another. One's word should never be given lightly, Scoop would tell his troops, but once given it should be one's bond. "Never play loose with the truth" was another favorite piece of advice. Incapable himself of lying, Jackson was shocked when he encountered someone lying or artfully prevaricating. On the rare occasions when he opposed a President's nominee to an appointive post, it was usually because of his doubts about the individual's veracity.

There was nothing of the ideologue in Jackson. Those seeking his support in political campaigns were not required to pass litmus tests of doctrinal purity. His helping hand went out to Southern conservatives, Northern liberals and Western in-betweeners alike.

But on issues concerned with America's fundamental values, or with the nation's security and survival, what Britain's great parliamentarian, Edmund Burke, said when he spoke to the Electors of Bristol in 1774, could have easily been said by Henry Jackson in 1974. "Your representative owes you, not his industry only, but his judgement; and he betrays, instead of serving you, if he sacrifices it to your opinion. . . ."[4]

So it was when Jackson stood up to the late Senator Joe McCarthy, who, under the guise of rooting out subversives in the government, was doing injury to countless innocent people. McCarthy had convinced many Americans that his charges were well-founded. President Eisenhower had declined entering the lists against the junior Senator from Wisconsin, and important office holders who had criticized McCarthy's methods had seen their political careers ended or endangered.

Therefore, it took political courage on the part of Jackson and a number of other Senators to serve on a Select Committee that in precedent-breaking, nationally televised hearings weighed McCarthy's charges that the Army was infiltrated by communists and subversives, and which ended by concluding there was no evidence to support McCarthy's extravagant allegations.

In his Presidential runs of later years, Scoop would again define his responsibilities in Burkean terms. He found it necessary to continue adhering to national security views differing from those of constituencies within his party without whose support he could scarcely hope to become the Democratic standard bearer. He really could not have done otherwise—Henry Jackson was a patriot who simply could not take positions that he was convinced would endanger his country and its values.

His patriotism was not of the chest-thumping kind that views America as the best of all possible nations. On the contrary, as far ahead as he could peer, he saw for his nation an unfinished agenda of business that needed doing, and problems that needed solving. But he also saw his country as one in which the good far outweighed the bad. So if he found no call for jingoism, neither did he find any reason for self-flagellation.

Jackson viewed his country in much the same way that Shakespeare had viewed his—naught shall make us rue if to ourselves we rest but true. He profoundly believed that the strengths of our system were such that there was no challenge we could not meet—provided we always did our best. And maybe that is what Scoop Jackson was really all about. He did his best to help his country do its best.

The Jackson Subcommittee on National Security

GRENVILLE GARSIDE

Grenville Garside has been a partner in the Washington, D.C., law firm of Van Ness, Feldman, Sutcliffe and Curtis since January 1979. He is also Vice President and a member of the Executive Committee of the Henry M. Jackson Foundation.

From 1959–1960, he was a professional staff member of the Subcommittee on National Policy Machinery, chaired by Senator Jackson. He returned to serve as Legislative Counsel to the Senator 1969–72, moving in 1972 to the professional staff of the Senate Committee on Energy and Natural Resources—which was chaired by Senator Jackson—to coordinate its study of National Fuels and Energy Policy. From 1975–79 he was Staff Director and Counsel to the Committee on Energy and Natural Resources. He had previously been Special Assistant to the Secretary of the Interior 1967–68. AB 1952 Princeton University; LLB 1959 University of Virginia.

Shortly after beginning his second term in the Senate, with the Eisenhower administration into its seventh year, Senator Henry Jackson spoke to the National War College about the perils of the Cold War and the challenge posed to the free nations by the rise of world communism. The overriding national issue of that time was the confrontation with the Soviet Union and Jackson was not at all sure that the country was prepared to carry on the struggle, as he described it, "to determine what kind of world system is to be created on this planet, a communist world system or a world system where free institutions can survive and flourish."

Jackson saw the nation facing an unprecedented military, scientific and political challenge from Moscow and questioned whether we had a coherent and purposeful strategy to respond. This led him to question the policy process and mechanisms which he thought had failed to produce the kind of national strategy our world position required. Jackson was particularly critical of the National Security Council, charging that it was a "dangerously misleading facade" which "spends most of its time readying papers that mean all things to all men."[1]

Scoop realized that the Cold War placed new demands on government agencies and their leaders, but knew there had been no comprehensive study of national policy-making machinery since the National Security Act was passed by Congress in 1947. He decided there should be one, and

the Senate responded to his initiative in July 1959 by authorizing a study of the organization of the Federal government
for carrying out policies for the "solution of the problems of
survival with which the free world is confronted in the contest with world communism." Or, as Senator Jackson put it
on the Senate floor on July 14, 1959:

> The study provided for in Senate Resolution 115 is directed to
> this fundamental issue: Can a free society so organize its human
> and material resources as to outthink, outplan and outperform
> totalitarianism? Can a free society so organize itself as to recog-
> nize new problems in the world and in space—and respond in
> time with new ideas?[2]

The study was to be conducted by a Government Operations subcommittee called by the improbable name of the
Subcommittee on National Policy Machinery. Created in
1959, it survived in one form or another for almost fifteen
years, spanning the administrations of three Presidents.
The Subcommittee changed its name twice. In 1962, it
became the Subcommittee on National Security Staffing
and Operations and in 1965 the Subcommittee on National Security and International Operations. Hereinafter,
it is simply referred to as "the Subcommittee." Its members included Hubert Humphrey, Edmund Muskie and
Jacob Javits. It remained, however, the highly personal
venture of the junior Senator from Washington. Its ranking Republican throughout this period was the genial conservative, Senator Karl Mundt of South Dakota. At an
early stage, Scoop consulted with and brought Karl Mundt
into camp, made him comfortable as part of the operation,
and the Subcommittee became and remained a bipartisan
venture.

Jackson selected a small but experienced staff headed initially by J.K. Mansfield, who had worked closely with him on the Joint Committee on Atomic Energy, and then by Dorothy Fosdick, who had served on the Policy Planning Staff at the State Department and became for some twenty-eight years Scoop's closest adviser on foreign policy issues. Key consultants included Oberlin Professor Robert W. Tufts, who also had served on the Policy Planning Staff, and Professor Richard E. Neustadt of Columbia, who later directed the Institute of Politics at the Kennedy School of Government at Harvard.

THE NATIONAL SECURITY COUNCIL

The Subcommittee initially focused its studies on the formulation of national security policy, with particular emphasis on the National Security Council (NSC). During the Eisenhower administration, the NSC apparatus had been greatly enlarged with the creation of a Planning Board and an Operations Coordinating Board. The NSC staff was assuming functions which had been performed by the Departments. The Council was considering a growing number of issues and generating an increasing number of position papers. The question that concerned Jackson was whether all this activity was producing policies responsive to the Soviet challenge. In his 1959 National War College speech, Jackson had said: "Why did it take a letter from the Congress as late as 1955 to induce the President to receive his first full-scale briefing on the status of our ballistic missile program? . . . What we need and what we are looking for is a national policy-making system that by its nature gets critical issues, sharply defined, up to the highest level where a conclusion can be reached on them—in good time."

The very prospect of a study of policy-making at the Presidential level made the White House nervous and led to negotiations between Scoop and the White House which produced "guidelines" for the study (i.e., it would not get involved in the substance of NSC policies) and a letter of endorsement from President Eisenhower.

Jackson was realist enough to know that unless the press and public became interested in the inquiry, meaningful results were unlikely. He was determined to stage a set of public hearings calling upon witnesses whose experience and knowledge of the national security policy-making process were beyond question. And he aimed to come up with findings and recommendations that would be useful to occupants of the White House following President Eisenhower.

For six months, under Jackson's direction, the staff interviewed and consulted widely, staking out the areas and issues of the inquiry. The Subcommittee's public phase began on February 23, 1960 with testimony from Robert A. Lovett, the former Secretary of Defense and Under Secretary of State. Jackson's selection of Lovett was no accident. A confidant and close adviser to George C. Marshall, Lovett had proved himself in a series of demanding national security posts over many years. His stature as one of the "wise men" of American leadership in the postwar period was unquestioned. This austere Eastern Establishmentarian was an urbane, witty and powerful witness. His appearance gave the Subcommittee instant credibility.

Ranging across a number of issues raised by the Chairman and his fellow Senators, Lovett called for restoring the authority of individual executives, in particular the primacy of the Secretary of State as first adviser to the

President in foreign policy. In his inimitable style, he argued that the derogation of individual authority and the "exaltation of the anonymous mass, has resulted in a noticeable lack of decisiveness." He attacked the proliferation of committees in the national security field, arguing that they "have become positive menaces to the prompt and orderly conduct of business."[3]

Over the next months, the Subcommittee heard testimony from an array of witnesses representing the world of business, science and government. They were, according to a *New York Times* correspondent:

men whose experience and knowledge and motives are beyond any challenge of pettiness or partisanship, and an ominous consensus has emerged from their testimony. It is that the mechanics of policy planning at the highest level have been made obsolete . . . that vital policy decisions are often extemporized, or based on inadequate information, or constricted by habits of thought that have been outmoded; and, finally, that there is a failure at the top policy level to sense either the magnitude of the threat facing the country or the immensity of the effort needed to combat it.[4]

Jackson in particular sought the views of current and former Secretaries of State and Defense, Special Assistants for National Security Affairs and Directors of the Policy Planning Staff at State. Their testimony ranged over the spectrum of national security decision-making and because of their extensive experience with the policy process, gave added weight to the Subcommittee's findings and recommendations.

The Subcommittee's work confirmed Jackson's view that the NSC was not functioning as it should to define issues for the President and give him creative ideas that could lead to new policy initiatives. Scoop perceived the vital importance of a President being fully informed, having the benefit of hearing diverse views debated in his presence so he could think through the full implications of a policy before adopting it. He thought the Council should serve this purpose by providing an intimate forum where the President could discuss a few critical issues with his chief advisers and relate his decisions to a coherent national strategy. The NSC could not fulfill this role, however, because it was becoming over-institutionalized and bureaucratic.

The Subcommittee zeroed in on the NSC bureaucracy, in particular the Operations Coordinating Board which was supposed to follow through on NSC decisions. "Actually," a staff report concluded, "the OCB has little impact on the real coordination of policy execution" but its existence "creates a false sense of security" that the execution of policy was being properly coordinated.[5]

It turned out that President-elect Kennedy used the Jackson Subcommittee staff report on the National Security Council (December 12, 1960) in effect as his transition study on the NSC. On January 1, 1961, in announcing the appointment of McGeorge Bundy as his Special Assistant for National Security Affairs, the President-elect said:

I have been much impressed with the constructive criticism contained in the recent staff report by Senator Jackson's Subcommittee on National Policy Machinery. The Subcommittee's study provides a useful starting point for the work that Mr. Bundy will undertake in helping me to strengthen and to simplify the operations of the National Security Council.[6]

Kennedy had been in office barely a month when he signed an Executive Order abolishing the Operations Coordinating Board.

Jackson also concluded that radical changes in existing policy machinery were unnecessary. The Subcommittee rejected proposals for "super-Cabinet" officers (e.g., a First Secretary of Government for national security and foreign affairs standing between the President and the Cabinet) and "super-staffs" above the departments in the national security field. Following Mr. Lovett's advice, it also crusaded against the proliferation of committees. The Subcommittee had counted some 160 interagency committees in the foreign affairs field alone. It touted Averell Harriman's proposal for a "committee-killing outfit" to identify committees which were good candidates for extinction, suggesting that the Bureau of the Budget give this task high priority.

In its reports, the Subcommittee put heavy emphasis on the importance of people in the policy process—the need for recruiting men and women with experience and good judgment to serve the nation. While Jackson believed that good organization was important, he was also convinced that good people could triumph over faulty organization. He greatly respected men like Robert Lovett, Dean Acheson and John McCloy, the lawyers and investment bankers who served with such distinction in national security posts in the postwar years. He considered their experience in the private sector invaluable training for their later government service because it involved "skill and shrewdnesss in judging the competence of advisers, in sensing when to have confidence in expert testimony and when not to. It is a skill that comes from dealing with people, rather than with numbers or things or production lines."

Clearly, Jackson had these citizen-leaders in mind when he said in a final statement on the first phase of the

Subcommittee's work in November 1961 that the key "problem of national security is not reorganization—it is getting our best people into key foreign policy and defense posts."[7]

THE SECRETARY OF STATE

The Subcommittee's work on national security policy-making led inevitably to a central focus on the crucial role of the Secretary of State. Jackson was concerned that the Secretary and his Department were not asserting needed leadership. He thought the Department had not kept pace with the tremendous growth of foreign policy activity in the postwar period. It was not doing enough to coordinate these activities and develop new policies through serious forward planning. There is, he wrote, "no satisfactory substitute for a Secretary of State willing and able to exercise his leadership across the full range of national security matters, as they relate to foreign policy."[8]

Between 1962 and 1964, the Subcommittee focused on the role of the Secretary of State and his Department in the policy process as well as the role of U.S. Ambassadors and their missions. Witnesses included David K.E. Bruce, W. Averell Harriman and Edwin O. Reischauer. This study recognized the dilemma of the modern-day Secretary in seeking to fulfill the demanding roles of advising the President, running the Department, representing his country overseas and serving as principal foreign policy spokesman. It was too much for one man, yet there was no easy way to delegate or ignore these responsibilities.

All the more reason, the Subcommittee concluded, that the Secretary of State needed a strong, well-staffed and well-run Department. The Subcommittee received cogent testimony, including that of Secretary of State Dean Rusk, about the problem of "layering" in the Department. It called for a determined effort to consolidate overlapping functions, trim staff, abolish committees and give responsibility to individuals.

Senator Jackson was particularly aware of the crucial nature of the relationship between the President and the Secretary of State. To be effective, the Secretary needed to enjoy the unusual respect and support of the President. The staff reports emphasized the mutual obligations of both men. The Secretary has a duty to "assert his own position and exercise his proper interest across the whole contemporary front of foreign relations." At the same time, the President "should be careful not to ask other officers to handle independently tasks which fall within the jurisdiction of the Secretary of State."[9]

Ambassadors needed help too. The modern Ambassador was expected to perform traditional diplomatic functions "in a most untraditional setting, with less independence and less policy authority than Ambassadors once exercised—and with far more people under foot." (At least 44 American agencies were represented at the Embassy in London). The Subcommittee concluded that Ambassadors would be helped by more clearcut, timely policy signals, by better backup in Washington (e.g. faster response to communications) and more discretion as to how best to approach the governments to which they were accredited.[10]

One outgrowth of the State Department study was the Subcommittee's sponsorship of a State-Defense Officer Exchange Program. The idea of a temporary exchange of outstanding civilian and military personnel between the two Departments to broaden their experience was first suggested in an early Subcommittee staff report. Secretary of State Herter later endorsed the concept in Subcommittee testimony after his staff and Jackson's had informally worked out the details of the proposal. With Jackson's support and Subcommittee backing, a pilot exchange was started and a successful program continues today.[11]

The Subcommittee's interest in having people of more breadth and experience in national security posts was later reflected in an unusual publication in 1968 called *Specialists and Generalists*. Rarely has a Senate Subcommittee sponsored a document which included comments by Aesop, Plato, Machiavelli and Hans Christian Andersen. It turned out to be a best seller. In the introduction to this collection, Jackson made clear where he stood in the specialist versus generalist debate. There is, he wrote, "no substitute in government for the wise generalist with skill and shrewdness in judging the competence of specialists and in determining the operational feasibility and political acceptability of any plan of action."[12]

THE ATLANTIC ALLIANCE

The Subcommittee gave Jackson wide latitude for addressing the foreign policy problems that were of special interest to him. The Atlantic Alliance is a case in point. At a time when the nation was increasingly preoccupied with Vietnam, Jackson in 1965 undertook a Subcommittee study of decision-making by the Atlantic Alliance to focus attention on the problems of NATO which was then undergoing severe strain.[13]

The Subcommittee mobilized a distinguished group of witnesses to testify—including Dean Acheson, Lauris Nor-

Henry M. Jackson

Congressman Jackson and Senator Warren G. Magnuson with
President Harry Truman at White House bill signing, 1949.

Softball on a Georgetown, D.C., playfield in the mid-1950s, with catcher Senator John F. Kennedy and umpire Senator Mike Mansfield (UPI photo).

Scoop returning from a submarine cruise, accompanied by Vice Admiral Hyman G. Rickover, 1959.

Chairing a hearing of his National Security Subcommittee, the
Senator consults with staff aides J. K. Mansfield and Dorothy
Fosdick, 1960 (George Tames, *New York Times*).

The Senator on an inspection visit to U.S. Army troops stationed in Nuremberg, 1969.

Senator Jackson and Helen Jackson meeting with Premier Zhou
Enlai in a Beijing hospital, 1974.

Scoop at a White House "working lunch" with President Jimmy
Carter, Vice President Walter Mondale, Assistant to the President
for National Security Affairs Zbigniew Brzezinski, and Senators
Edmund Muskie and Abraham Ribicoff, 1977.

Senators Jackson, Ted Stevens, Jacob Javits, and Claiborne Pell during discussions with President Anwar Sadat at his villa on the Nile.

Scoop talks with students at the School of International Studies (now the Henry M. Jackson School of International Studies), University of Washington.

A welcome opportunity for uninterrupted study.

Senator Jackson introduces Aleksandr Solzhenitsyn to Senate colleagues, U.S. Senate, 1975.

Senator Jackson and family meeting with Prime Minister Menachem Begin in Jerusalem, 1979.

Henry Jackson and Deng Xiaoping, the Great Hall of
the People, Beijing, 1983.

Senator Jackson and President Ronald Reagan, the White House, 1983.

Scoop in his study at home in Everett, WA (Greg Gilbert, *Seattle Times*).

stad and John J. McCloy—largely in support of shoring up the Alliance. It was Jackson's strongly held view that American forces in Europe should not be reduced, as some were then proposing. He made sure that this point was hammered home at the hearings. In a not untypical exchange with McCloy in May 1966, Senator Jackson commented on the need to understand "what is wise policy in the present situation when NATO is trying to meet the shock of the French withdrawal" and asked McCloy to comment. McCloy responded that

this would be a most inappropriate time to reduce those forces. If at this stage, coincidental with the French attack on NATO, we pull out a substantial number of our troops, I think that the cat would be among the pigeons and it would probably be the death knell of NATO. I cannot see that it would be a wise policy to take any such steps.[14]

After making a solid record with this kind of testimony, Jackson would then use the ammunition to counter efforts underway in the Senate to vote reductions in U.S. forces in Europe.

Jackson later observed that the most important finding of the Subcommittee's Atlantic Alliance study was the "urgent need to improve the practice of Alliance consultation." Because sovereign states do not have to agree, "consultation is the decision-making process, the substitute for executive authority," and "the only means available to clear up differences of view and to arrive at agreement on a common course of action."[15] The art of consultation came naturally to Scoop, whose diligence and skill at consulting his colleagues was a key to his success as a legislator.

The Atlantic Alliance study took the Subcommittee into

the field of international diplomacy and set the stage for a 1969–1970 inquiry into the process and problems of international negotiations. Scoop had become deeply interested in the art of effective negotiation and how to keep lines of communication open, particularly with adversaries. At a Subcommittee hearing in April 1970, he emphasized the need to understand the other side as clearly as possible, pointing out that in negotiating with the Soviet Union, "we need to be up-to-date on what is really going on in the Soviet Union and what the Soviet leadership is thinking and doing."[16]

The Subcommittee went about its negotiations study with characteristic thoroughness. It invited testimony from two noted British authorities on the Soviet Union (Robert Conquest and Leonard Shapiro), commissioned papers by distinguished experts on the effectiveness of the U.S. in negotiating with communist powers and published informative collections of documents discussing the Soviet and Chinese approach to negotiations. These papers included a pioneering analysis of the problems of negotiating scholar exchange programs with the Soviet Union.[17]

The negotiations materials also included some advice from Robert Lovett which Scoop particularly liked. Lovett had said:

> I do not think there is any such thing as a "self-policing treaty," or "self-enforcing treaty" between two countries without similar ideas of law, order and political freedom. The right of inspection between two parties who distrust each other is essential. . . .
>   Avoid, if possible, any negative pledge. . . . In fact, don't use "never" in your commitments.[18]

U.S. policy-makers would do well to heed this advice today.

THE CONTINUING EDUCATION OF THE CHAIRMAN

While the Subcommittee had an influential impact over the years, it seems clear that the Subcommittee experience also significantly shaped the style and thinking of its Chairman.

Unquestionably, prolonged participation in the Subcommittee's studies deepened Scoop's knowledge and understanding of foreign and national security policy-making. Over several years, despite heavy responsibilities in other areas, he immersed himself in the substance of the Subcommittee's work, talking to experts and reading papers on subjects which included conflict of interest laws and systems analysis in the national security field. Having his own staff on hand to discuss issues and pursue answers helped sharpen his thinking. He relied on the staff not only for Subcommittee work but also to assist on other foreign policy matters in which he was involved, including arms control and human rights.

The Subcommittee also brought Scoop into close touch with a group of talented Americans whom he might never have encountered in the normal course of his Senate service. This included not only Subcommittee witnesses but also other government officials, academic experts, investment bankers, businessmen and generals. It soon became clear that he had developed an extraordinary "talent bank" to which he could turn for advice and counsel and he used it.

Scoop had already achieved recognition in the national security field when the Subcommittee was created and his stature was further enhanced through its work. Campaigning for Kennedy as Democratic National Chairman in 1960, he drew heavily on the Subcommittee record. More than once he told the staff—with a twinkle in his eye—that Kennedy had complained to him he was talking too much about matters of national security. Of course, that didn't stop Scoop, particularly since he saw an opportunity in his role as National Chairman to influence the policies of the new administration.

Perhaps most important, the Subcommittee took Jackson outside the routine of the Senate to view the world from the perspective of the White House. He developed a feel for the Presidential viewpoint. He discovered more about the ins and outs of the Departments of State and Defense and other national security agencies than some of their leaders ever did. He saw how policies might be advanced, thwarted or corrupted in the labyrinthian maze of the executive branch.

Thus, the Subcommittee experience profoundly enhanced Scoop's understanding and perception as to how a President might overcome the hazards of making and carrying out sound national security policies. In this respect, the Subcommittee not only sharpened his skills as a Senator, it must also have strengthened his confidence that he could be a successful President.

A President he was not to be, but as Chairman of the Subcommittee, he made a record that remains today a model of innovative and constructive legislative leadership.

Jackson: Foreign Affairs Generalist

JAMES ROCHE

James G. Roche has been Vice President and Director of the Northrop Analysis Center in Washington, D.C., since January 1984.

He first worked with Senator Jackson as senior professional staff of the Senate Select Committee on Intelligence April 1979–February 1981, returning in January 1983 as Director of the Staff for the Minority of the Senate Armed Services Committee when the Senator became the ranking member.

He is a retired Captain in the U.S. Navy. Before joining Senator Jackson he served as Assistant Director, Office of the Secretary of Defense (Net Assessment) October 1975–April 1979. From February 1981–January 1983 he was Senior Deputy Director of the Policy Planning Staff, Office of the Secretary of State. BA 1960 Illinois Institute of Technology; MS 1966 U.S. Naval Postgraduate School; PhD 1972 Harvard Graduate School of Business Administration.

Sometimes foreign policy is learned in the classroom, sometimes it's learned in meetings with some of the world's leaders, and sometimes it's learned in the quiet perusal of a thoughtful book. Sometimes, in the case of Senator Jackson, it was learned in the rain.

It didn't seem to fit the image at all. Somehow, one would have expected that the Senator would have been more comfortable sitting in a big leather chair discussing the state of the nation's defenses. But here he was, 68 years old, with his wife and two children, staring at the Russians in the company of military officers from the Norwegian northern command.

They probably didn't even know that he was there. But, as the small boat motored slowly down the Norwegian side of the river that constituted the border in that part of the North Cape region, he relished the fact that he had once again traveled above the Arctic Circle to the outposts of freedom. He didn't wish to provoke the Russians—he was always cautioning Presidents, Cabinet Officers, and Senators against unnecessarily taunting the Soviets. His purpose was to get a sense of what it was like to be toe-to-toe with the Russians on a daily basis, to learn a little bit more about them. And when he spoke to the Norwegian border troops he met, he wanted them to know how proud of them he was, how proud of his Norwegian heritage he was, and how important he thought they were to the preservation of freedom.

Henry Jackson was a foreign affairs generalist. He distrusted "specialists" who viewed problems only from a very narrow perspective. He was wary of military officers who didn't have the breadth to understand geopolitics. And he had no confidence in foreign service officers who didn't appreciate the nature and the impact of the military balance in the world. "Professor Jackson" repeatedly pointed out to his staff of "students" that to understand any interesting problem in public policy, one had to imbed it in a larger context. Thus, throughout his career Jackson brought a broad foreign policy perspective to the consideration of military programs. Although people talked about him as Secretary of Defense in more than one administration, he wasn't really interested. The only Cabinet position that had any attraction for him was Secretary of State. Actually, in 1968 President-elect Nixon asked him to join his Cabinet as Secretary of Defense. Scoop declined. He was then offered the post of Secretary of State which, for the Senator, was more difficult to turn down since, next to the Presidency, he viewed that office as the most important in the land.

Jackson's heroes were seasoned civilian leaders, and included men like the able investment banker, Robert Lovett, who had served the nation in both the Department of State as the Under Secretary, and in the Department of Defense as Deputy Secretary, and later as Secretary.

In his pioneer 1960 inquiry on organizing for national security, with Robert Lovett as the lead witness, Jackson emphasized the inseparable nature of national and foreign policies and defense planning, and the need to understand basic policy in order to do military planning successfully.

In discussions of military programs and budgets the Senator persistently probed their foreign policy implications. He wanted to understand how some nuclear system was going to contribute to deterrence. And he wanted to know how major conventional forces and systems were to contribute to conventional deterrence of Soviet or Soviet-client adventurism. When he saw proposals for military systems, or uses of military forces, which failed to make foreign policy sense, he didn't hesitate to criticize them.

Thus, the Senator who was renowned for standing by America's friend, Israel, strongly criticized the deployment of U.S. Marines to Lebanon in 1982. But the same Senator stood alone among his colleagues in the Senate minority in 1983, and praised the use of American military forces deployed to deter Libya from attacking the Sudan as a "textbook example" of how to use military forces to achieve political goals.

In some respects, one can understand what Senator Jackson wanted for America by understanding what he valued in people. Thus, he liked men and women who exhibited strength of character, who were steady and reliable, who had good judgment and common sense, who had the courage of their convictions, and who kept their word.

Jackson wanted an America that was strong enough to deter its adversaries and help protect its friends and allies. In an era of nuclear weapons, he wanted an America that was steady so that its actions would be predictable and its word could be accepted by its friends and adversaries alike. He wanted an American government that exercised good judgment and took actions that made sense to the people of the world. And he wanted an America that was courageous enough to stand by its friends and allies in times of troubles, that would speak out with firmness when it saw abuses of human rights by powerful as well as weak nations, and that would quietly warn its friends and allies when they followed policies that undermined freedom.

STRENGTH

The helicopter had taken off from one of Her Majesty's Royal Naval cruisers well off the coast of Scotland. It had flown into the Royal Air Force Base to pick up the Senator and one of his aides. It was not a "VIP" helicopter, but an operational bird designed primarily for anti-submarine operations—as clean as an operational war fighting system should be. This was not a problem for Scoop. The young British pilots didn't quite know what to make of the Senator, but they did know that London considered him very special. Not being familiar with legislators, let alone American ones, they were a bit surprised when he took the helmet offered him, and climbed aboard with his usual smile and enthusiasm. Once in the air, he and they hit it off. It was a magnificent day, unlike so many in the north of Scotland at that time of year, so they took him on a little tour of the fjords along the way.

When the helicopter finally arrived at Faslane he was welcomed by a gathering of very senior British submariners. The Senator told the admirals that he had asked to be taken on a tour of the area so that he could get a better understanding of the lay of the land. And with a wink and a wave to the young pilots, he walked off to a briefing room to have a to-the-point, classified, professional discussion of submarine operations in the Norwegian Sea. While his hosts were impressed with his knowledge of the Soviet navy, they seemed amazed by his ability to discuss the long-range plans for Her Majesty's Royal Submarine Force.

In the *New York Times Magazine* of August 4, 1963, Senator Jackson noted that: "As I read history, international peace and security depend not on a balance of power but on a certain imbalance of power favorable to the defenders of peace—in which the strength of the peacekeeper is greater than that of the peaceupsetter."[1] To the Senator this did not mean that the U.S. had to have more tanks or troops than the Soviets (after all, even in the early 1960s the Soviets had far more conventional forces than did the U.S.), but that the West had to maintain a full spectrum of deterrence against all forms of Soviet aggression, about which neither we in the West nor the Russians could have any doubt. For him a robust military deterrent was critical if the U.S. was to lead the West. He often characterized Soviet strategy as being like a burglar in a hotel who goes from door to door; when he finds a door locked, he moves on; but when he finds a door unlocked, he enters.

The Senator was profoundly concerned about regional conflicts where the U.S. was unclear about its vital interests, and where the Soviets, or one of their client states, might take action leading to U.S. involvement and the possibility of superpower conflict. This meant two things. *One,* the U.S. had to understand what its vital interests really were. Having done this, it meant keeping our public statements in line with our willingness to commit forces. If possible, we could encourage allies to take up the slack, or if we were doing a good job of intelligence, we might be able to help the potential victim of Soviet adventurism

with arms and other military assistance. *Two,* it meant
fielding credible conventional forces, including the means
to lift them by air and sea to project U.S. power as needed.
He was concerned that the Soviets might miscalculate and
make a move based on their assessment that the U.S.
lacked forces which it could put in place in time to deter
attack.

While he was deeply concerned about regional conflicts
getting out of hand and leading to superpower conflict, he
knew that the basis of the nation's deterrent, even its
conventional deterrent, was its nuclear forces. If this component of the defense program atrophied, then no number of conventional forces, at whatever level of quality,
could deter the Soviets. He understood that the essential
issue was deterrence, and that the nuclear weapon was a
trump card that could serve as a compensatory deterrent
for shortcomings in a nation's conventional posture.

At the same time, he staunchly opposed excessive or
unnecessary reliance on the use of nuclear weapons. Thus,
he was strongly opposed to the withdrawal of U.S. forces
from Europe, pointing out to his fellow legislators during
debate in 1971:

> The sizable cutback of American troops proposed in this
> amendment would imply a greater reliance on nuclear weapons
> and their incorporation in military operations at a very early
> phase of hostilities. Is this what sponsors of the amendment really
> want? Are they in favor of a one option policy of massive retalia-
> tion? Would this serve the best interests of the United States and
> its allies? Hardly! We must not leave the American President with
> only the nuclear button in his hand in the event of crises.[2]

In early 1956, on the floor of the Senate, the Senator
said that "American superiority in advanced weapons systems is the minimum prerequisite of peace. Without such

superiority all our other programs for staying Soviet power will prove in vain."[3] He fully understood that the nuclear deterrent preserved the peace, and gave our allies the incentive to maintain even the minimum conventional force structure. Over time, as it became apparent that the Soviet Union had the capacity as well as the will to field many more nuclear weapons than the United States might, he recognized the diminishing marginal value of simply adding more and more nuclear weapons to our stockpile. Therefore, he vigorously argued for the maintenance of "essential equivalence" in nuclear capabilities, and especially in the maintenance of a portfolio of forces—the land, sea, and air triad—whose strength depended on the invulnerability of the portfolio rather than on the survivability of each and every component.

By the time the Senator had become the ranking minority member of the Senate Committee on Armed Services in 1983, he had seen the ups and downs of the defense budget. In the late 1970s he had been one of the leaders in causing the administration to increase the amount of resources devoted to defense. He had seen the gradual decline in America's combat capabilities after the Vietnam War, and began increasingly to worry about the state of the deterrent. Speaking in 1980 to a Coalition for a Democratic Majority Friends of Freedom Awards Dinner in honor of Andrei Sakharov, he said:

Only a strong America can stand up to the Soviet Union, safeguard the interests of our friends and allies, combat terrorism, champion human rights, and conduct wise and steady diplomacy. My friends, we can prove by the coming votes on the defense budget that a confident America is embarked on a long-term bipartisan effort to restore the balance of power. Nothing would do more to hearten our friends and allies abroad. Nothing would do more to give hope to those in the USSR who are resisting Soviet oppression and aggression. And nothing would do more to assure that the free peoples of the world—and not the tyrants—will inherit the future.[4]

The key 1980 votes for the defense budget on the floor of the Senate did go his way; for the first time in anyone's recent recollection the legislature forced money on the President for the nation's defenses. Scoop also made his views known to President-elect Reagan as a member of the President-elect's Foreign Policy Advisory Board. By 1983, there had been major increases in the defense budgets.

STEADINESS

Jackson was in the House of Representatives when NATO was formed. He was still in the House a year later when Dean Acheson, as Secretary of State, came up to the Congress and told the members that it was necessary to place American troops in Europe, in fact in Germany, in order to deter Soviet aggression there. The Senator always understood that forces-in-being were necessary for deterrence; a generalized commitment made verbally just wasn't the same. And so he found himself defending the deployment of these forces time and again. He wanted the allies to do more for their own defense. He didn't like some of the things our allies felt all too free to say about America. And he was sympathetic to his colleagues' arguments that the U.S. taxpayer was carrying a heavy burden of defense expenditures, as well as balance-of-payments problems. To help his colleagues and the American people understand the value of steadiness in our commitments to the NATO Alliance, he chaired a series of major open hearings on the Atlantic Alliance in the mid-1960s and initiated a number of studies and published reports.

In a 1966 speech on the Senate floor the Senator summed up his view:

> The main purpose of the U.S. troop commitment in Europe is to leave the Russians in no doubt that the United States would be involved if they attacked Western Europe—making it clear to the Russians that they would meet enough U.S. troops to make it a Soviet-American crisis, not just a European one. . . .
>
> The function of these American troops, together with European troops, has been, and continues to be, to meet a local crisis as effectively as they can, posing the continual threat that, if the crisis continues and enlarges, the danger of . . . war continues and enlarges with it. That policy is as valid today as it ever has been. It has also been effective. It has closed the door to Soviet westward expansion. No armed attack has been made on Western Europe or North America. Moreover, what justifiable hope there is of a genuine European settlement rests, I believe, on the constancy of this policy. . . .[5]

Seventeen years later Scoop was still making the same relevant arguments.

There's an interesting sidelight to Jackson's legislative defense of our deployments in Europe. From 1966 on through 1971, Scoop and Senator Mike Mansfield fought head-to-head over one version or another of the "Mansfield amendment" calling for a substantial reduction of U.S. forces stationed in Europe. The words were often strong, and forcibly stated, but one of Jackson's virtues was that he was able to keep policy differences separate from personal differences, to "disagree without being disagreeable." So no one was really surprised that, when Ronald Reagan won the Presidency, Scoop quietly obtained a commitment from the new administration to keep his former policy adversary, Mike Mansfield, as the U.S. Ambassador to Japan.

For Jackson, being steady also meant standing by one's friends.

In 1956 Scoop went to the Soviet Union for a first-hand look, travelling as far east as Alma Ata in the China-Xinjiang border area, visiting Tashkent and Samarkand and exiting through Afghanistan. He always hoped for a return visit, but his championship of international human rights, including the right to emigrate, apparently reduced the opportunity of a Soviet welcome. It was not until 1978 that the Kremlin leadership, for their own reasons, invited him to Moscow to talk to Secretary Brezhnev. Jackson happily accepted. In the course of discussing arrangements with Soviet Ambassador Dobrynin in Washington, D.C., the Senator indicated that while in Moscow he would want to pay his respects to Dr. Andrei Sakharov and have a brief, private talk with a small group of Soviet citizens who had applied to emigrate. Such quiet get-togethers in Moscow with American Senators and Congressmen were not at all unusual and in deference to Kremlin nervousness the Senator emphasized that his talks would be out of the limelight. The message came back from Moscow that unless the Senator gave up these plans, his trip was indefinitely postponed. Since Scoop had no intention of meeting with Secretary Brezhnev in the Kremlin and totally ignoring his friends, that was that. The Soviets cancelled the invitation, and another was never extended.

The Senator expected America to be loyal to its friends and allies. This was clear in his consistent stand on NATO even during those times when some of our European friends were almost insufferable. Then there was Israel.

He would point out that the United States only had one
ally in the Middle East that it could rely on, and that was
Israel. (He considered Turkey a member of NATO, and
lived torn between his affection for the Greeks, and his
understanding of the critical role of Turkey in the Alliance.) Israel was a democracy; it was the only representative government in the area; and its democratic character
was fundamental for him as an affirmation of his deeply
held belief in individual liberty and social justice. Its people worked hard and were competent. It had effective
armed forces, and a proven capacity to defend itself effectively when challenged. Thus, Israel deserved our support—even when times were rough. Jackson's consistently
stated point was that it was in America's interest to support
Israel.

Scoop used to laugh at some of the so-called sophisticated people in Washington who allowed themselves to
believe that Congress was controlled by a powerful Israeli
lobby. He used to say: "These people just don't understand. They refuse to realize that the *American people* support Israel. Americans, whether gentile or Jew, respect
competence. They like the idea that we are on the side
which seems to know what it's doing." When Israel attacked the Iraqi nuclear reactor facility, he knew that the
American people would approve—no matter how much
the State Department carried on about it. He was right.

One of his joys was to sit down with Israeli generals and
discuss military and political issues of the Middle East. He
was always curious about Israel's reserve system that could
multiply its standing forces dramatically in 48 hours. And
he was interested in Israel's military infrastructure which
we might use if the U.S. had to enter the area in a serious
way. He believed that no other country in the region

would stand by us in the event we had a conflict with Moscow. You stand by your friends.

Scoop, of course, did not always agree with the Israelis. His disagreement with Israel over settlement policies on the West Bank became public in the late 1970s. He had held these views for some time, and had communicated them to the Israeli government in many ways and on many occasions. There were other disagreements over Israeli military policies, but his views were conveyed in private, as he considered fitting for a friend hoping to be helpful. No matter how much he disagreed with the government of Israel on this or that policy, he thought it wrong to punish Israel either by denying the appropriate means for her to defend herself, or by arming her deadly enemies. To his way of thinking, it isn't smart to give sophisticated weapons to those countries who intend to use them primarily against your friends. As long as the Soviets were giving arms to Arab states who remained in a state of war with Israel, it was incumbent on the U.S. to stand by Israel. Thus, Scoop was especially delighted when Egypt made peace with Israel, and he extended the same hand of friendship to the Egyptians, who, like the Israelis, naturally took to him.

For Scoop the quality of steadiness meant that the United States should maintain its equilibrium even when it found itself in deep trouble. And the Vietnam War became deep trouble. Long concerned that Indochina not slip into the totalitarian orbit, the Senator had supported the Southeast Asia Collective Defense Treaty in 1954— while not a treaty of the force of NATO. He saw the threat to the region as in part military, but also political and economic—as in so many vulnerable Third World areas. He believed that the peoples of Asia and Africa are not likely to be saved to the free world in the long run unless they want to save themselves and take primary responsibility for doing it.

For years the United States had given limited military aid to help support the French-Vietnam forces in holding off the divisions of the communist Vietminh. But with the collapse of the French Indochina effort at Dien Bien Phu, the South was increasingly vulnerable to the forces of the North, and the U.S. role in the area inched up. In the tradition of rallying behind a President in a foreign policy crisis, the Senator supported President Kennedy when he deployed his Green Berets and President Johnson when he sent additional American forces into South Vietnam. Once U.S. troops were committed in the field, Scoop stood loyally behind them and focused his efforts on helping sustain bipartisan support for the U.S. undertaking.

At the invitation of Secretary of the Army Cyrus Vance, Jackson flew to South Vietnam in December 1962 for observation of the counter-insurgency effort, helicopter visits into the fighting areas, and talks with U.S. commanders and troops. Again in December 1965 he flew out for an on-the-spot evaluation. That time, he included an inspection of the Da Nang Civilian Hospital, by then totally manned with volunteer American doctors and nurses under the auspices of Project Hope, and woefully short of desperately needed supplies. It seems no previous visiting American politicians had responded to the repeated appeals for help. In characteristic fashion, Scoop immediately adopted the hospital as a special concern. On returning to Washington, D.C. he saw to it that the urgently required medicines were promptly dispatched on their way. He then drafted Senator Stuart Symington, who some months later was headed for Saigon, to check up on how things were going at the hospital and to see if more supplies were needed.

As the Vietnam War dragged on and on, with the United States getting into deeper and deeper difficulties, Scoop refused to join those who in one way or another simply wanted "to pull the plug" without any regard to the consequences. In his words: "As I see it, American disengagement from Vietnam must be phased and orderly, or our foreign policy problems will become more unmanageable than ever."[6]

As a result of standing by the President and trying to help him, Scoop found himself widely labeled by the pejorative word "hawk." As the record shows, this was a serious oversimplification of Scoop's position on this complex matter of foreign policy and national security.

A White House meeting not widely known about even today took place following Hanoi's Tet offensive. Senator Richard Russell, Senator John Stennis and Senator Jackson, together with Clark Clifford, meeting privately with President Johnson at the White House, strongly opposed the President's attempt to commit a quarter of a million more American troops into Vietnam and persuaded him to withhold this proposal. "I opposed it," Senator Jackson said, "because we must start to wind this thing down."[7]

Meanwhile, Scoop concentrated his personal efforts on building congressional and public support for a negotiated settlement that would permit the staged withdrawal of U.S. troops. In 1968 he had proposed that "high on the agenda of any talks should be a mutual cease-fire—a stop to the fighting on both sides, to end the killing and the bloodshed and the destruction."[8] Time and again thereafter, working with a volunteer citizens group called

"Cease-Fire Now," the Senator pressed the White House for the strongest possible political and diplomatic effort to achieve a standstill cease-fire. These efforts culminated on September 1, 1970, with a bipartisan letter to President Nixon joined in by Senator Hugh Scott and 28 other Democratic and Republican Senators, urging the administration to propose a mutual, internationally supervised, standstill cease-fire throughout Vietnam to end the killing and the war, and to achieve a return of prisoners of war, and the conduct of prompt, open, free and fair elections.[9] This cease-fire initiative was adopted as American policy by President Nixon in an October 7, 1970 address.

A year later Jackson said, "If there is a lesson of Vietnam, it's that a great power like the U.S. simply can't get involved in a situation, no matter what the circumstances might be, that's going to involve a long, drawn out, protracted war of attrition."[10]

Scoop's instincts were correct that the subjugation of South Vietnam by North Vietnam with the consequent threat to all of Indochina should be resisted—both for geopolitical and human rights considerations. He knew the right objective, but he was realistic. We had done what we could with the support of only a few allies. We had held out for a long time. The political will of the U.S. was not there to match the tenacity of the adversary in his form of unconventional, guerrilla warfare. We could not continue to bear the human and domestic political costs of a war of attrition. We had to extricate ourselves. The alternative would be to go in with even far larger forces, and this was politically unacceptable. So we did what we could to arm and train the South Vietnam forces. Their forces were not strong enough, however, to resist those of

North Vietnam which proceeded to overrun South Vietnam and Laos—and then Cambodia, where a local despot
was replaced by a conquering army.

It was no surprise to Jackson that the National Liberation
Front (NLF), thought by many to be more than the North
Vietnam front that it was, ceased to exist within hours of
Hanoi's successful invasion of Saigon. He had anticipated
that when the North Vietnam leadership came to power
there would be terror, murder, re-education camps, and
uncountable refugees. But the wholesale, continuing tragedy of Indochina is more terrible than anyone expected.

When counseling Presidents and others in subsequent
years, Scoop's experience of the Vietnam War caused him
to emphasize: think it through, understand what the full
impact of your actions may be, don't act too quickly, and
keep steady.

JUDGMENT AND COMMON SENSE

As he entered the Chinese Embassy in Washington, D.C.,
it was obvious that Jackson was going to be greeted like a
long-lost relative. He had come for a private dinner with
the Deputy Chief of Mission, and had brought along some
of his aides. It was the late 1970s when verbally beating-up
on the Soviet Union was grand sport for U.S.-Chinese
gatherings. One would have expected Russian-bashing of
the highest caliber, mixed with appropriate digs at the
Soviet lackey Vietnam. While the Vietnamese government
did come in for its fair share of verbal assaults, it might
have been surprising to some that the Senator emphasized
the point that "we must understand the real nature of the
Russian threat, and we must be very careful not to go
around needlessly provoking them." His hosts, who acted

as if they were in the company of someone who knew the Soviets as well as they did, agreed with him.

For Jackson, military power was but one aspect of a nation's strength. The Senator clearly understood that economic health and social and political well-being were critical to any society's long-term stability. When he examined a situation like the conflict in Central America he knew that there was no such thing as a "military solution." He recognized that, at best, military force could provide little more than a shield against outside intervention. However, behind this shield, a country had to take those social and political initiatives that would allow its citizens to develop and prosper.

In considering the Soviet empire, Scoop recognized that the Russians' primary strength was their military arm, and that they would rely on it to control the people under their domination. This would be the case, in his view, because the Soviet economic and social models simply could not succeed. The Senator had no doubt that Eastern Europe would remain a potential flashpoint as long as the Soviets chose to keep it under their domination. And he recognized immediately after the invasion of Afghanistan that the Soviets would have to take years, and extraordinary means, if they were to bring the people of that country under their rule.

Jackson believed it necessary to the preservation of peace that both sides keep talking, and that the U.S. look for those situations where the interests of both sides converged, and work with the Soviets in those cases. And he understood that communications included more than private diplomatic exchanges. There were times for strong language to be used in public, and there were times for restraint in the statements of senior officials. He was very sensitive, moreover, to the different roles of various American officials in speaking of the Russians. There was an obvious difference to him between a Senator denoucing a Russian move, and unnecessarily provocative rhetoric and name-calling by senior administration officials. The difference was in the weight the Soviets placed on the pronouncements of one Senator as compared to an official of the executive branch, especially if the official were the President or the Secretary of State.

Good judgment was very important to Scoop. Like Diogenes with his lamp, the Senator valued honesty, but beyond this he was always looking for what he called "people with good judgment." He explained it this way:

> In policy-making, of course, there is no substitute for sound judgment, and sound judgment depends not only on the relatively common quality of courage but also on the rarer quality of steadiness, on the capacity to consider in cool detachment the end of any road before starting out on it, on a sense of knowing when to act and when to be patient, and on skill in using advisers and expert help. Really sound judgment seems to depend upon experience.[11]

For Scoop, a sense of history was another condition of good judgment. Peter Jackson, speaking of his father, recalls: "Whenever we talked about how things were going at my school, he would always ask how much history I was taking—the message was perfectly clear."[12] Many a government official received a variant of this message. His fellow Senators would sit back and smile when Scoop began to ask some confident foreign policy, intelligence, or defense official about the backdrop to the current crisis which had brought the expert to the witness stand. His colleagues smiled because they knew that, nine times out of ten, Scoop was going to have to give the official a gentle but thorough history lesson.

The Senator liked to apply to any situation what he termed "basic common sense." He was an early and staunch advocate of the ballistic-missile-firing, nuclear-powered submarine based on geopolitical logic and a common-sense understanding of the distinctive role of underwater strategic nuclear forces. He argued for such programs as the cruise missile and the Advanced Technology Bomber as military investments the U.S. could make to cause the Soviets to divert more of their military resources toward less-threatening defense programs.

Sometimes the Senator judged that a minor or neglected project deserved his attention: these came to be known as Scoop's orphans. For example, in 1984 when the new headquarters for the Defense Intelligence Agency was dedicated, both the Secretary of Defense and the Director of the Agency spoke of only one man: Senator Henry M. Jackson. The proposal for the building had languished in the Congress year after year. But in 1980 it became his "orphan of the year," and he fought successfully to get it funded. His logic was simple and sensible: if you want a first-rate intelligence service to complement and compete intellectually with the CIA, and be able to attract the very best young scholars, then you don't house its analysts in buildings whose ceilings quite literally were falling down!

Scoop had been close to the world of intelligence for most of his time in the Congress because of his duties on the Joint Atomic Energy Committee and the Senate Armed Services Committee. He knew the history of the community like few of its members. Little is known publicly about Jackson's tenure on the Senate Select Committee on Intelligence, and that is the way it is supposed to be. Unlike other committees, membership on this Committee does not lead to public exposure, or at least it's not supposed to. Scoop was an energetic member of that Committee, but few people were aware of his influence. Not so the intelligence community.

Whether it was in consideration of issues of treaty verification, or national technical systems, or the value of covert operations, those members of the intelligence community who didn't do their homework found themselves up against "the old prosecutor from Everett." Often he started questioning a witness with the "I don't know anything about this stuff, I'm just an old prosecutor from a small town" routine. When some proposal for covert action struck Jackson as plainly stupid, he said so. And many an idea went back to the drawing board because it just "didn't make sense, speaking in geopolitical terms."

Jackson understood that military and intelligence capabilities were as dependent on good people as was the national security policy process, on which he had directed so many fruitful hearings. Therefore, he was very concerned with the morale of the members of the armed forces. And he was particularly concerned with the nation's capability to attract and keep some of its best minds in intelligence. He was convinced that neither wise foreign policy nor sensible military planning could be conducted on a shallow intelligence base. So he worked continuously to improve the analytical capabilities of this community, and especially its ability to reach out and work with informed scholars in this country and the West more generally. "People," he would say, "it always comes down to people."

COURAGE

Some of his fellow Senators couldn't understand it, especially those who didn't know him well. They thought if only they had a chance to talk to him, he would see it their way. After all, they prided themselves as civil libertarians, and the Senator sitting across the table from them defending his position that there had to be limits on the expanded use by the government of the polygraph device was not known as "soft on the Russians." "In our efforts to uncover the spies," he told them, "I'm concerned that the innocent be protected from the misuse of this inherently unreliable machine." It was a fight every step of the way, but, in the end, Jackson had a provision enacted into law which declared a moratorium on the expanded use of the polygraph device in the Defense Department.

Not long thereafter, President Reagan withdrew the National Security Decision Directive which had authorized the expanded and widespread use of the machine in the government. One of the Senator's younger colleagues on the Armed Services Committee said afterwards that the finest thing the Senate Armed Services Committee had done in 1983 was to have the courage to stand up for the civil liberties of the men and women who worked for the Defense Department. Only after Scoop's death was Defense able to begin to get its way on the expanded use of the polygraph. Even then, however, his wisdom lived on in the close scrutiny and the many constraints his former colleagues, especially Senator Sam Nunn, applied to the Department's plans.

Jackson had the courage of his convictions. And he expected those around him to have the courage to stand up and champion wiser policies—but to do so within the rules. That was his way: don't just complain, do something about it if you can.

In the late 1970s the Senator had a new aide join him, and to this newcomer he assigned the task of doing an analysis of whether or not the Boeing Company (headquartered in his home state) should be allowed to sell transport aircraft to Libya. He was especially interested in the issue of Libyan support of terrorism ("Is it really as bad as some would have us believe?"), and he wanted recommendations as to what position he should take. The aide was given no indication of how the Senator "was leaning." Two days later, with some trepidation, the aide returned to the Senator with a finding that Libya clearly supported international terrorism, and that, consequently, he recommended the Senator oppose the pending Boeing sale. Scoop listened with his deadpan look, then smiled and gave what the aide would learn was the highest Jacksonian compliment: "Good work. That's what I think, too." It was a great day for me.

The Senator and
American Arms Control Policy

RICHARD N. PERLE

Richard N. Perle became Assistant Secretary of Defense for International Security Policy in March 1981.

He served in professional staff and advisory positions with Senator Jackson from October 1969 into 1979, on the Jackson Subcommittee on National Security and International Operations, Senator Jackson's personal office, and the Permanent Subcommittee on Investigations, seconded for a period to the Subcommittee on Arms Control, Senate Committee on Armed Services.

He began his career in government in June 1969, first working for the Committee to Maintain a Prudent Defense Policy, then as full-time consultant to the Special Assistant to the Secretary of Defense. Just prior to becoming Assistant Secretary of Defense he was a consultant for several corporations. He has authored or co-authored numerous articles dealing with foreign policy issues facing the United States. BA 1964 University of Southern California; MA 1967 Department of Politics, Princeton University.

If Scoop Jackson's view of
arms control had been as simple as his critics thought,
they might have understood it. But it was, in fact, a complex blend of historical insight, a sense of the nature of
totalitarian rule, a feel for the subtleties of the negotiating
process and the common sense with which he treated all
things.

Scoop would have regarded the idea that he was an
implacable opponent of arms control as foolish as well as
mistaken. Mistaken because he had voted for every arms
control agreement to be reported to the Senate for a final
vote during his service there, a fact that a few minutes
with his long record would have revealed.[1] And foolish
because it makes no sense to be *for* or *against* arms control
in the abstract. One is for or against specific agreements,
specific terms within them, specific provisions. Competent
Senators don't vote on abstractions; they vote to give advice and consent to treaties or otherwise to sanction agreements made by the executive branch. And it was with the
specifics that Scoop was always concerned.

THE JACKSON APPROACH

Jackson knew the specifics better than anyone else in the
Senate. Knowing the details was part of his job. He worked
at it very hard. He could master detail without becoming
bogged down in it; and while his command of the facts

seemed effortless as he spoke on the Senate floor or interrogated a witness at a hearing, it was the product of intense study. He had little patience for those of his colleagues who became lyrical in speeches about arms control
or peace or national security when he knew they hadn't
the slightest grasp of the specifics of the issue at hand.
During the debate on the 1972 ABM Treaty and the Interim Agreement on Offensive Arms—a debate that went on
for several weeks on and off the Senate floor—he never
tired of pointing out to his colleagues that he, and not the
Foreign Relations Committee (or its Chairman, William
Fulbright), had explored the details of the agreements in
hour after painstaking hour of hearings in the Committee
on Armed Services. It was Scoop who had asked the prob-
ing questions, plumbing the ambiguities, the loopholes,
the imprecision that would later affect so profoundly the
impact of the agreements on the strategic forces of the
signatories, and become a source of bitter controversy.

There was a pattern to Scoop's self-defined role, as a
Senator, in the formulation of arms control policy and as a
leader in the legislative disposition of treaties and agreements that were brought before the Senate. It was, in a
word, to improve them; to press the executive branch
departments—State, Defense, the Arms Control and Disarmament Agency, the National Security Council—to
think longer and harder about the specifics, about verification, about negotiating tactics, than they were likely to
do if he, or someone like him, was not watching every
move. Even when he was counseling Presidents and Secretaries of State and Defense he was deeply conscious of the
bureaucratic milieu in which arms control policies were
developed. And he was superbly well informed, the result,
in part, of the regard in which he was held by executive

branch officials who sought his advice and counsel and readily shared with him the factual knowledge he needed to influence their departments.

The knowledge in the executive departments that any treaty they might negotiate would have to earn the support of two-thirds of the Senate, and that doing so would be virtually impossible without Jackson's support, made Scoop a repository, as well as a dispenser, of opinion and information. People came to him from everywhere, telling as well as asking. If there was a battle between executive departments Scoop was likely to know about it long before it made its way up to the Cabinet level. A crucial issue about to be decided at the NSC? Scoop was almost certain to know in time to counsel one course or another. Information that didn't come to him informally from a multitude of officials could be elicited at hearings at which he consistently managed to know what questions to ask.

Scoop Jackson became so central to the arms control process because he knew more about it than other members of Congress, Senate or House, and more than Cabinet officers who wandered on the scene for two or three years. They came and went. Scoop was there decade after decade through the administrations of Roosevelt, Truman, Eisenhower, Kennedy, Johnson, Nixon, Ford, Carter and well into Ronald Reagan's first term. Never more than once would a Cabinet officer try to get through a hearing at which Scoop was present by a last-minute read through the briefing book. With Jackson present and asking questions the world would know if you didn't command the subject, broadly and in detail. Military officers, in particular, would learn more about arms control by preparing for an appearance before Jackson's Subcommittee on Arms Control (of the Armed Services Committee) than at any other time in their career. They might coast through the executive inter-agency deliberations with only a passing knowledge; but take the witness seat in front of Scoop and you had better know what you were talking about.

All of this was done, of course, without histrionics, without shouting. Just persistent questioning aimed precisely at the point he wished to make. Witnesses would often race frantically through their well-tabulated briefing books, temporizing with long-winded obfuscations until they would find that the page wasn't there. The questioning would end with a sheepish, "Senator Jackson, I will have to supply that for the record."

These encounters at hearings only strengthened the impression of his colleagues, congressional staff and the press that Scoop knew more about the subject than the Cabinet secretaries who came to testify. The secretaries would appear in the hope of persuading the Senators. But so often they would leave behind a committee or subcommittee more convinced than ever that it was Scoop's knowledge, judgment and experience on which one could count.

When it came to interrogating executive branch witnesses Scoop had no equal. "Never," he would say, "ask a question unless you know the answer." He wasn't about to be surprised. Perceptive witnesses soon learned that if Scoop inquired about a document the chances were he had a copy; if he asked about a meeting he probably knew what had gone on. Evasion was pointless. Double-talk wouldn't work. Only the ten-minute rule gave you any comfort at all—and that was only a respite. Scoop would be back again when his turn came, picking up where he had left off.

During the course of a negotiation the point of all this was to shape the decisions and policies of the executive branch, and sometimes to prepare the ground for legislation. Once an agreeement was reached and laid before the Senate the interrogation became part of the effort to influence the ratification debate. That might mean building a coalition to insist on reservations or on some associated program of activity without which the agreement would place national security interests at risk.

THE LIMITED NUCLEAR TEST BAN TREATY

In the 1963 debate that surrounded the Atmospheric Test Ban Senator Jackson had pressed the hard questions: what would the United States do if the Soviets were to break out of the Treaty, conduct a series of tests and then announce a resumption of the Treaty terms? They had done something rather like that in 1961 in connection with the bilateral U.S.-USSR moratorium on atmospheric nuclear tests, and Scoop was determined that we should be protected against a repeat performance. What would we do to maintain a vigorous test program when only underground testing was permitted? Could—would—we maintain the Los Alamos and Livermore laboratories and the Nevada test establishment if nuclear tests in the atmosphere were no longer permitted? Scoop hammered away at these questions, gathering in a group of Senators whose votes were crucial to ratification. And then he began to negotiate with the administration. What resulted was a series of four safeguards, agreed to by the Kennedy administration, that would accompany the Treaty if it was ratified. The labs would be maintained. We would maintain readiness to resume testing should the Soviets do so. We would test underground. And we would improve our capability to monitor compliance and respect for the terms of the Treaty. With the safeguards agreed to, Scoop and several Senators, with whom he had made common cause by organizing them into a decisive bloc, voted to ratify the Atmospheric Test Ban. He had demonstrated that it was possible to combine arms control and national security by a careful balancing of restraint and readiness.

When I began to work for Scoop in 1969 one of my first assignments was to prepare the annual report he made to the Senate on the implementation of the four safeguards. Scoop watched over them, mindful of how easy it was, with the Treaty in place, to forget the necessity for a vigorous testing program underground in order to improve safety, security, survivability, reliability and effectiveness of our nuclear weapons. What had looked, during the hearings and the ratification debate, like opposition to the Limited Nuclear Test Ban Treaty from the junior Senator from Washington became the basis for an improved and more balanced outcome in which ratification was not defeated but assured.

THE SAFEGUARD ABM SYSTEM

In November 1969 a U.S. negotiating team led by Gerard Smith travelled to Helsinki for the first round of the Strategic Arms Limitation Talks. Scoop knew that the key to a successful negotiation was support in the Congress for the major elements of the administration's strategic program. The most controversial among them was deployment of an anti-ballistic missile defense system known as Safeguard and planned for deployment around Washington, D.C.

and at a dozen other locations. When in place the Safe-guard system would serve to protect the National Command Authority against an accidental or unauthorized or third country attack. And it would protect a significant fraction of our land-based deterrent, our Minuteman missiles, against even a substantial Soviet attack.

From the beginning of the SALT negotiations the Soviets insisted that they would only agree to limit their offensive forces if we agreed to limit our freedom to deploy defenses. Scoop was tireless in marshalling support for the deployment of Safeguard. He organized and led the Senate supporters, a Democrat throwing his weight behind the deployment plans of a Republican administration whose ranks he had declined to join as Secretary of Defense and as Secretary of State.

"In matters of national security," he used to say, "the best politics is no politics." Party lines meant nothing to Scoop where national security was concerned. Indeed, so strong was his conviction on this point that his Democratic colleagues knew that the argument least likely to move him was a partisan appeal. In Jackson's presence no one would suggest a party-line vote on a defense issue. Alongside his nonpartisan commitment to national defense they would be embarrassed to suggest it.

As with matters of arms control Scoop became the Senate's expert on anti-ballistic missile defense. He worked hard, engaging staff and technical experts for hours on end, reviewing Defense Department reports, studying the statistics, giving advice and counsel. His office became a virtual command center for the debate over ABM in 1969 (and again in 1970 and 1971).

Scoop knew that without Safeguard the SALT I negotiations would fail. And he was determined that that must not be allowed to happen. When the final roll call ended a bitter Senate debate Scoop was in the well of the Senate managing the vote, watching over his brood like a mother hen. Safeguard was approved by a single vote in 1969 and from President Nixon to NSC Adviser Kissinger to Secretary of Defense Laird to his colleagues in the Senate they all knew who had done it.

THE INTERIM SALT I AGREEMENT
AND THE JACKSON AMENDMENT

Having sustained the Safeguard system through the Senate Scoop was understandably dismayed when President Nixon returned from Moscow in May 1972 with an Interim Agreement on Offensive Arms that permitted the Soviets a level of offensive weapons higher than that of the United States. Safeguards had been bargained away in the ABM Treaty in order to "halt the momentum of the Soviet offensive buildup." But far from halting the Soviets, the Interim Agreement allowed Soviet forces to expand. The Agreement allowed the Soviets to keep all of their 308 heavy missiles (the United States had none) and to continue to add warheads by the thousands to their missile force of 1,618 land-based intercontinental missiles and up to 950 submarine-launched ballistic missiles. (The corresponding figures for the United States were 1,054 and 656, respectively.) This amounted to a fifty percent Soviet advantage in land-based and a thirty percent advantage in sea-based ballistic missiles.

Scoop voted to ratify the ABM Treaty. But he set about finding a way to improve on the Interim Agreement—or, at the very least, to do what he could to insure that the inequalities that favored the Soviet Union would not be repeated in any permanent treaty when the Interim Agreement expired in 1977. To lay the foundation for what was later to become the Jackson amendment to the Interim Agreement authorizing resolution (as the Interim Agreement was not a treaty it needed an "affirmative Act of Congress" to be approved), he began an extensive set of Armed Services Committee hearings aimed at clarifying the many ambiguities of the Interim Agreement and developing the theme that the unequal ceilings it provided were not acceptable in any future treaty.

Hour after hour, week after week, Scoop interrogated the administration officials responsible for arms control and the negotiators themselves. Where the Interim Agreement was imprecise he sought to get administration witnesses to state a clear American interpretation. Where there were discernible loopholes he prodded administration spokesmen to say how the United States would react if the Soviets were to exploit them by taking actions that ran counter to the sense of the Agreement. To this day the record of those hearings, in several volumes, together with the floor debate on the Jackson amendment, constitute the clearest and most authoritative guide as to the meaning— the rights and obligations under—the Interim Agreement on Offensive Arms.

With the meaning of the Interim Agreement clarified, Scoop offered his amendment. It put the Senate (it was later adopted by the House and signed into law by President Nixon) clearly on record that any future agreement on offensive arms must "not limit the United States to levels of intercontinental strategic forces inferior to the limits provided for the Soviet Union."

I can recall the morning the Jackson amendment was made public. After many hours of secret negotiation the

Nixon administration had agreed to support the amendment. It was co-sponsored by Senator Scott of Pennsylvania, then the minority leader of the Senate, and Gordon Allott of Colorado, Chairman of the Republican Policy Committee—to leave no doubt as to where the administration stood. Senator Fulbright was on the floor of the Senate when someone brought him a copy of the *New York Times* for August 3, 1972.[2] It carried a front-page story by the *Times* defense correspondent, William Beecher, the gist of which was that Scoop had an amendment to the authorizing resolution, that it was being supported by the administration, and that it provided the above language as well as a declaration that a failure to achieve a follow-on Treaty by the end of 1977 that would protect the survivability of the United States land-based missile force could jeopardize our supreme national interests. This latter phrase linked the Interim Agreement to the ABM Treaty which allows for withdrawal on six months' notice in the event of a threat to our supreme national interests. Finally, the Jackson amendment called for a vigorous program of research and development leading to the modernization of the United States strategic force.

Fulbright, the *Times* article in front of him, was stunned. He expressed doubt that the story could be true. Senator Alan Cranston entered the Senate chamber and announced that he had just spoken with a member of Scoop's staff, who had confirmed the story. The fight was on.

For six weeks the Senate debated the Jackson amendment. For six weeks Scoop argued the principle of equality—in warheads, in weapons systems, and in throw weight—the carrying capacity of ballistic missile forces. Scoop's mastery of the details of the Treaty were evident from the first hour of that debate. With John Tower and Gordon Allott and a handful of others he argued for his amendment against Senators Fulbright and Church and Javits and Percy and Muskie and Cranston and a great many others. And as the debate wore on the number of Senators co-sponsoring the amendment grew daily. When the roll was finally called, on September 14, 1972, almost four months after President Nixon returned from Moscow with the Interim Agreement in hand, the Jackson amendment was approved by a vote of 56 to 35. The euphoria that had greeted Nixon on his return from Moscow when he spoke to a joint session of Congress had given way to a far more sober reflection on the nature of the Interim Agreement and the risks involved in any administration bringing home a treaty that authorized the Soviets a larger number of strategic weapons than the United States. A new standard of precision had been established as the administration learned that there was no question it could expect to leave unanswered as it sought the advice and consent of any Senate in which Scoop Jackson was a member.

Scoop knew that his amendment would dampen enthusiasm that might otherwise lead to a permanent treaty that left the United States with less than parity in strategic weapons. And he knew that it would temper the administration's extravagant claims that the Interim Agreement had yielded an accommodation with the Soviet Union that would justify diminishing the importance of modernizing America's strategic deterrent. But he could not have known that fourteen years later, in a negotiating session that lasted all night in Reykjavik, Iceland, Ambassador Paul Nitze would say to Soviet Marshal Akhromeyev that the United States could not agree to a less-than-equal

ceiling on strategic forces because the Congress of the
United States had spoken to this issue and had insisted on
equality in any future agreement. And he could surely not
have known that, after conferring with the Soviet leadership at three in the morning, Marshal Akhromeyev
would concede the point and agree to equal ceilings on
Soviet and American strategic forces at sharply reduced
levels. As I listened to the Soviet Marshal, Chief of the
Soviet Armed Forces, I could feel Scoop smiling over the
proceedings.

THE SALT II NEGOTIATIONS

From 1972 through the conclusion of the SALT II Treaty
in 1979 Scoop monitored the progress of the United
States-Soviet arms control negotiations with intense concern. He did not wish to be surprised by an agreement he
could not support.

Having fought long and hard to assure that any SALT
II Treaty would provide for equality, Scoop embarked on
an extended series of hearings in the Subcommittee on
Arms Control of the Armed Services Committee aimed at
following the evolution of the negotiations and influencing
their course. For the remainder of Nixon's time in office
and during the Ford administration he continued to emphasize two themes: equality and reductions. Arguing that
the SALT I Interim Agreement authorized a massive Soviet build-up of strategic forces—a build-up that began
before the ink was dry and continued without pause—
Scoop pressed for reductions in every hearing, every briefing, every press conference and in a number of speeches
on the Senate floor. Sometimes his advice was of a general
nature; sometimes it was highly specific.[3] More than once

he proposed a schedule of reductions that would have diminished strategic forces by a third or more down to an equal ceiling.

While neither Nixon nor Ford, both of whom permitted Henry Kissinger to formulate policy on arms control and, in all essential respects to manage the negotiations, followed Scoop's advice, Scoop knew that he was framing the context in which any SALT II Treaty would be evaluated when it came to the Senate for ratification. He understood well the importance of "making the record." That his advice was often ignored mattered little alongside the importance of framing the issues and the debate. Like a justice on the Supreme Court who believes that a strong and cogent dissent is a vital part of the long-term process of making constitutional law, Scoop believed that the record of his views and those of the administration officials whom he interrogated at hearings would form a vital part of the long-term development of an American arms control policy. It was a challenge of which he never tired, even when results seemed remote and the task endless.

In November 1974 President Ford and Leonid Brezhnev reached a general framework agreement at Vladivostok. Scoop was wary of such general outline agreements. The Soviets had perfected the art of eliciting a general agreement while subsequently vitiating much of its structural integrity in the laborious, detailed negotiations that followed. Western publics, always keen to see the general agreement translated into a signable treaty would lose patience and the Soviets could count on concessions on essential details. Thus the one issue left vague and uncertain at Vladivostok and later settled through diplomatic channels after Ford returned to Washington was resolved in favor of the Soviets; after ten days of waiting to see the text of the agreement reached at Vladivostok the administration, no longer able to explain why it could not produce a text, gave in. Scoop drew the appropriate lesson.

The holdover issue had to do with limitations on cruise missiles with a range over 600 kilometers. The limitation, which Ford and Kissinger had resisted for ten days, eventually became part of the SALT II Treaty and, in Scoop's view, one of its most objectionable provisions since it affected United States cruise missiles in Europe (banning them for a two-year period in a protocol to SALT II) while permitting the Soviets to keep an unlimited number of ballistic missiles with even greater range and capability with which to threaten Europe and American troops stationed there. Thus, for the duration of the SALT II protocol at least, the Soviets were able to exploit an asymmetry that invited the deployment of the SS-20 missiles that were later to dominate the discussion of arms control well into the Reagan administration.

The Vladivostok agreement was never concluded in treaty form by the Ford administration which came to an end without the SALT II Treaty that was foreshadowed there. It fell to the Carter administration to carry on where Kissinger and Ford had left off.

Shortly after Carter took office in January 1977, Scoop sent him a lengthy, carefully reasoned memorandum detailing his criticism of the Soviet position then on the table in the aftermath of Vladivostok. It was read by the new President as a critique of the Soviet negotiating position. It was in fact a critique of the thinking that had developed in the closing months of the Ford administration and, in particular, the views of Henry Kissinger. Scoop thought that the Ford administration was inordinately concerned with the "negotiability" of the American position in the

SALT II talks, ruling out sound positions on the grounds that the Soviets would not accept them. Far better to stand our ground and to negotiate with patience and perseverance than to adjust one's position continuously in the face of Soviet intransigence—that was Scoop's view and it lay at the heart of much of his criticism.

Scoop's memorandum to Carter recommended holding out for deep reductions in SALT II, not settling for the formula that had begun to emerge from Vladivostok and that permitted massive Soviet increases under SALT II just as the SALT I Interim Agreement had permitted massive Soviet increases that Moscow had exploited fully. Looking back, it is difficult to fault Scoop's persistent advice. The Soviets eventually added some 8,000 strategic warheads to their arsenal pursuant to SALT I and to the unratified SALT II Treaty; and at the time of this writing they have yet to complete a building program that authorizes another 2,000 or so strategic warheads beyond that. This was not Scoop's idea of arms control; and he felt confident that he expressed the view of most Americans when he argued that arms control ought to entail reductions, not increases, in strategic arms.

How much of Scoop's memorandum recommending deep reductions in strategic offensive forces was taken to heart by President Carter is difficult to know. He sent it around to a number of his senior officials for comment and little is known of their reaction. Paul Warnke, whose nomination as Director of the Arms Control and Disarmament Agency Scoop had opposed, referred to it as "a masterpiece of advocacy." But it is doubtful that it advocated a policy that Warnke liked. The influence of Scoop's advice may have been at work when, early in 1977, Carter sent Secretary of State Cyrus Vance to Moscow with a proposal for sharp reductions in strategic offensive forces. The Soviets rejected the Carter/Vance Proposals out of hand, insisting on a treaty along the lines of the Vladivostok agreement. Scoop was disappointed—but not surprised—when Carter withdrew the deep reductions offer a mere six weeks after the Vance mission to Moscow. He had come to expect a lack of staying power among American negotiators, and he deplored it.

Scoop never made the contents of his memorandum to Carter public. He believed that private correspondence with the President was privileged. And while he used effectively the device of letters to the President that could be made public in order to achieve a political purpose, when it came to sensitive negotiating issues he appreciated the importance of confidentiality. A letter received from Carter in response, handwritten and outlining the new President's "objectives" for SALT II was also kept confidential by Senator Jackson. Even in the midst of the ratification debate on SALT II in which Scoop would come to play the central role, he never considered publishing the memorandum and the Carter letter in response. The temptation must have been great. For Scoop had, in early 1977, correctly anticipated the defects in the SALT II Treaty that would result if the new administration followed in the footsteps of the old—and it did. And the Carter response to Scoop would have been a powerful tool in the battle against ratification of the SALT II Treaty. Of the several "objectives" Carter had identified in 1977, fewer than half were realized in the Treaty he signed in 1979.

As the negotiations toward a SALT II Treaty proceeded under the Carter administration Jackson held frequent hearings with administration witnesses. Secretary of State

Vance was a frequent witness along with other officials involved in the negotiations. Scoop wanted to influence the course of the negotiations in the direction of deep reductions. And he wanted to build a record against the ratification of any Treaty that failed to achieve them or in other ways fell short in supporting U.S. national security interests. Disappointed as he was with the ease with which the administration had abandoned its reductions proposal in 1977, he tried through the hearing process to prevent a cascade of concessions on the many issues that divided the United States and Soviet negotiators.

As usual he kept in close touch with the evolution of the negotiations. When the issue arose of the Backfire bomber—a Soviet bomber capable of delivering weapons on the United States that the Soviets insisted was outside the scope of SALT II—Scoop chaired a five-hour hearing in which experts on the Backfire argued out the basis for their varying estimates of its range and payload. When the issue of cruise missiles was prominent in the negotiations he held hearings on the verification of cruise missiles, demonstrating that it was all but impossible to determine their range.

Verification was always a vital issue for Scoop. He didn't trust the Soviets to respect treaty provisions that could not be verified and he was deeply suspicious of the breezy confidence on the verification issue that various administration spokesmen expressed. In his relentless pursuit of the verification issue he developed many of the points that would later occupy the attention of the Reagan administration as it studied the Soviet compliance record and concluded that they had violated a number of provisions of the SALT II and ABM Treaties.

SALT II—THE RATIFICATION DEBATE

In June 1979 President Carter and Leonid Brezhnev, meeting at a summit in Vienna, concluded the SALT II Treaty. It contained a number of provisions that Scoop had counseled against during the five years that it was under negotiation. It protected a significant Soviet advantage in heavy missiles and ballistic missile throw weight. It did not include a direct limit on the number of Backfire bombers and the indirect limit that was contained in a side letter merely continued the production rate that the Soviets had already established. It lacked critical details on a number of crucial issues including baseline numbers of weapons and their characteristics against which future verification would be measured. But most disappointing of all it did not call for significant reductions in strategic weapons. And it included a two-year protocol that constrained the deployment by the United States of medium-range cruise missiles, a precedent for the future that Scoop feared would open the way to one-sided restrictions on medium-range weapons based in Europe. And like the SALT I Interim Agreement it was shot through with ambiguities that Scoop felt certain the Soviets would later exploit.

He lost no time in organizing hearings to explore fully the details of the new agreement. Hour after hour he interrogated administration witnesses—Secretary of State Vance, Secretary of Defense Harold Brown, the Joint Chiefs of Staff and the American negotiating team. He invited public witnesses to give their views and summoned a variety of former officials to testify.

Working closely with John Tower, the ranking Republican on the Armed Services Committee, he set about building the case that the Treaty ought not to be ratified.

In one memorable hearing Scoop questioned Defense Secretary Harold Brown on the provision of the Treaty that banned new types of ICBMs, a provision that the administration had argued would preclude the Soviets from proceeding with a fifth generation of such missiles. Behind him in the hearing room Scoop had a set of scale models of the currently-deployed Soviet ICBMs together with their successor fifth generation. Included, as a way of illustrating the comparative throw weight of the Soviet and U.S. missiles, were the American counterparts, dwarfed by the Soviet SS-18 and SS-19 missiles. When his turn came to put questions to Brown, Scoop placed the models on the desk in front of him and asked the Secretary of Defense to state whether the Soviets would be free to deploy each of them under the rule prohibiting, as the administration had claimed, the deployment of new types of ICBM. "Could they deploy this one?" Scoop asked, pointing to the new follow-on to the SS-18. "Or this one?" pointing to the follow-on to the SS-19. Brown was forced to concede that they could deploy these missiles, even if everything about them was "new." To other Senators on the committee it was a dramatic revelation of the extent to which the common sense meaning of the term "new" had been distorted in the Treaty beyond all recognition. It became evident that, despite administration claims, the Soviet fifth generation of missiles could proceed under the Treaty. A similar encounter with Secretary of State Cyrus Vance left him looking unpersuasive and ill-prepared to defend the administration's position. Both were forced to fall back on the flawed argument that while the Soviets might indeed go ahead with five new ICBMs their military utility could not significantly exceed the ones they replaced.

As testimony was given to the committee from its many witnesses, Scoop began urging his fellow committee members to prepare a report that would identify the many defects he believed made the Treaty unacceptable. Because the Committee on Foreign Relations had jurisdiction over the Treaty, a report was the best he could hope for. But he knew that a cogent, well-reasoned and documented report could have a profound effect on the consideration that would be given to the Treaty when it reached the Senate floor.

Repudiating the President on a matter as weighty as an arms control treaty with the Soviet Union is not a task that the Senate relishes. Even the preparation of a negative report by the Armed Services Committee would have been impossible if Scoop had not, over many years, explored the issues in a way that his Senate colleagues found persuasive and convincing. When the Committee did report, it was with the advice that the SALT II Treaty was "not in the national security interests of the United States of America," and it so found by a vote of 10 to 0 with 7 abstentions.[4] The committee report tracked closely the issues that Scoop had developed over the years.

The report of the Armed Services Committee together with the narrow vote favoring the Treaty by the Foreign Relations Committee indicated that the SALT II Treaty was in deep trouble in the Senate even before the Soviet's Christmas invasion of Afghanistan. A sustained lobbying effort by the Carter administration had failed to muster the two-thirds vote that was required for ratification. Scoop had succeeded in making the Senate aware of the deficiencies in the Treaty, especially the provisions dealing with heavy missiles, missile throw weight, new types of ICBMs, verification and the protocol limiting cruise missiles. These issues became the centerpiece of the debate that unfolded in the Senate as the administration delayed pressing for a vote it was certain to lose.

By the time the Soviet tanks rolled across the Afghan border after traversing the Termez-Kabul road—and President Carter had withdrawn the Treaty from the Senate docket—the United States Senate was well on the way to denying ratification of SALT II. Ironically, almost 25 years earlier, when he was shown the early construction of that highway then being built with Soviet assistance, Scoop had remarked to the American Ambassador to Afghanistan that that was the road by which the Soviets would one day invade. The same prescience, knowledge and geopolitical depth that led him to make that assessment in 1956 had enabled him to present a critique of the SALT II Treaty so comprehensive and convincing that his Senate colleagues, in numbers sufficient to deny ratification, understood that SALT II, rather than limiting the Soviet arms buildup, was in fact a license for the Kremlin to continue it into the fifth generation of their most threatening ICBM missiles. History has proved Scoop only too right.

Human Rights
and the Jackson Amendment

CHARLES HORNER

Charles Horner has been Associate Director (for Programs) of the United States Information Agency since December 1985.

He served in professional and advisory staff positions with Senator Jackson from 1972 to 1977 on the Subcommittee on National Security and International Operations and on the Permanent Subcommittee on Investigations.

Following membership on the adjunct faculty at Georgetown University's School of Foreign Service and associate of the Landegger Program in International Business Diplomacy, he was Deputy Representative to the UN Conference on the Law of the Sea in 1981, and then Deputy Assistant Secretary of State for Science and Technology from October 1981 to the fall of 1985. He has written on international issues for publications including *Commentary* and *American Spectator*. BA 1964 University of Pennsylvania; MA 1967 University of Chicago.

In 1974, the Soviet government had reached a self-generated crisis in its relationship with the greatest Russian writer of the century, Aleksandr Solzhenitsyn. And, whether in exasperation or by calculation, the Soviet authorities decided to expel him from his country. He was, in those days, a great and world-renowned celebrity, known through his writings, and through the force of his will as manifested in his ongoing struggles with the Soviet government on behalf of basic liberties. When Solzhenitsyn came to the United States in the summer of 1975, it seemed natural that he call on the President of the United States to offer a first-hand report from the front line of the human rights movement. But President Ford decided not to receive him. We learned later he had acted upon the advice of Secretary of State Henry Kissinger who, more or less, had let it be known that he thought of Solzhenitsyn as a threat to the administration's version of detente.

Senator Jackson, however, saw things differently. He believed Solzhenitsyn should be honored for his championship of human rights—and he undertook to do this by arranging a reception for him in the Senate Caucus Room on Capitol Hill.

Here, then, were two unlikely comrades-in-arms, the one an exemplar of a spiritual and literary tradition, almost opaque to one not steeped in it, the other the master American parliamentarian of indefatigably sunny disposition, certainly not prone to brooding. That these two men had come, literally, to embrace each other was noteworthy in its own right. Like Stalin's proverbial pope, neither commanded any divisions, but in the force of their personalities they had nonetheless managed to reduce the regimes of both superpowers to jelly. For, without a doubt, if one had surveyed the White House and the Kremlin in search of the men they feared the most, would one, in 1975, get an answer other than Henry Jackson and Aleksandr Solzhenitsyn?

As this is written, it is more than a decade since that event, but the real and symbolic persistence of the encounter between these two genuine, though wholly different, geniuses continues as an important fact of world politics. Solzhenitsyn is still a source of permanent discomfiture for those who deny the political meaning of his message. The powerful ideas propelled by Senator Jackson still influence the conduct of Soviet-American relations, still shape the debate over arms control, still—to focus on the subject here—compel reluctant officials to confront the connection between "human rights" and foreign policy.

In short, this is all rather extraordinary. How did it happen?

LAW AS A PROTECTOR OF INDIVIDUAL LIBERTIES

Jackson spent a year as a county prosecutor in the late 1930s, an experience which, over time, assumed a mythical role whenever he recounted his political history. He practiced law only briefly, but his profession of attorney was another frequent term of reference. Like some of his colleagues, he liked to begin a line of questioning at a hearing with the hoary disclaimer, "I'm just a country lawyer, but . . ." Other times, the tough prosecutor could be invoked. Though Jackson was not long a practicing lawyer, he nonetheless brought the training and higher sensibilities of his profession to his career as lawmaker.

For as much as Jackson later came to be termed by some "conservative" in his outlook, he was in fact steeped in the progressivism of the Pacific Northwest (James Farley did, after all, once refer to the forty-seven states and the Soviet of Washington) and in its particular notion that law was for the weak—weak individuals and weak nations. Indeed, the idea that the law exists to restrain the strong and protect the rights of the weak was at the core of everything Jackson did in the arena of international human rights. As a young prosecutor, Jackson gained a local reputation as a tough anti-fascist; as a veteran Senator, he seemed just as determined that international law in the grandest sense also serve as a protector of individual liberties. In this respect, there is a line which connected the humblest county ordinance to the loftiest of the United Nations pronouncements. The elaboration of the argument might become ever more sophisticated, but the living, breathing, individual human being was always the focus. Thus, while the encouragement of human rights on an international basis was put forward as a national obligation, it always seemed that Jackson had an instinct for the particulars of the situation—this man, that woman, a dancer in Leningrad, a poet in Cuba.

THE STRATEGIC SIGNIFICANCE OF HUMAN RIGHTS

Meanwhile, in the late 1930s, Americans faced a novel problem. For the first time since the war for independence, the rights of American citizens could conceivably

become jeopardized by the action of *foreign* powers. In
Germany and Japan, there arose powerful forces opposed
to the existence of democracy *on principle,* seeing the democracies of the Western world a mortal threat to their
own existence. The Soviet Union had a similar *theory* but,
in fact, did not then pose a comparable threat to the
liberties of other nations. Historians record the 1930s as a
time of extraordinary intellectual confusion on these
points. One senses, however, that for Henry Jackson,
about to begin four decades of congressional service, the
"world crisis" was the occasion for clarity. It seemed to
confirm what he had learned at home, and it provided a
remarkably consistent framework for both intellectual
analysis and political action.

Jackson often described his own first-hand encounter
with the full potential of totalitarian evil. He visited
Buchenwald shortly after its liberation, and learned the
meaning of the Holocaust as the central political experience of the century, a peculiar choice of terms perhaps,
but understandable in the sense that the Holocaust represented a total breakdown of law, politics, foreign policy,
humanity itself. Put another way, the Holocaust was the
result of an accumulation of grave lapses in understanding
the nature of anti-Semitism and totalitarianism, of ignoring the need both for military preparedness and strong,
effective foreign policies. After all, the response of the
world at large to the rise of Hitler was a contributor to all
of the subsequent horrors.

Yet, it was at about this time that the world faced another challenge to its understanding of history and politics. The tragedy of the 1930s, as Jackson well knew, was
the failure to understand the nature of the totalitarian
threat to the democracies—to understand the totality of

that threat. In the 1940s, we teetered on the brink of similar tragedy—an incipient failure to understand the threat posed by the Soviet Union. The degree to which the Soviets had replaced the Nazis as the primary threat to civilization—or whether they had indeed replaced them— was for many an unresolved intellectual and, therefore, political issue. Jackson's own Democratic Party, in an internal argument which foreshadowed the more profound divisions of twenty years later, was hardly of one mind on the subject. The Republican Party, for its part, had divisions of its own, and was not yet the committed internationalist party it was to become in later years. (How many remember, for example, that Robert Taft was one of thirteen Senators to vote against ratification of the NATO treaty?) For Jackson, the Second World War was a lesson in the relationships among geopolitics, strategic policy, military preparedness, international law and human rights. In the 1970s, when it was common to speak of "priorities," Jackson used to argue the interconnectedness of things, emphasizing that "success in one area will not overcome failure in another."

In 1968 Jackson first talked with Robert Conquest, the British author, and read his classic book, *The Great Terror: Stalin's Purge of the Thirties* (1968). That monumental work definitively described the terrible totalitarian excesses in the Stalin era—the bloody massacres, the suppression of whole peoples, the persecution of racial and religious minorities, the mass imprisonment of individuals for their political views—all sources of international instability and turmoil. The Senator was profoundly moved by the Conquest book: he recommended it time after time as "must" reading, driving home the point that a regime which engages in such wholesale violations of human rights at home would—more often than not—be a threat to its neighbors abroad and to international peace.

It is not surprising that Jackson enthusiastically raised the UN's Universal Declaration of Human Rights as his flag and standard. In reading the basic UN documents one is once again struck by the connection they establish between democratization and international peace. Indeed, the Charter makes it clear that at least one proper—if not the only proper—definition of "peace-loving" nation is in fact "human-rights-respecting" nation. For a government's treatment of its own citizens, especially the government of a *powerful* nation, is an indication of its intentions toward the rest of the world.

Thus in the Senator's view, human rights and international law—usually viewed as humanitarian, or at best, political, concerns—were strategically significant. In this, he and Andrei Sakharov found themselves soulmates. Jackson never tired of quoting from one of Sakharov's messages from Moscow:

> I am convinced that there are certain guarantees for the political and civil rights of man that cannot be separated from the main tasks before mankind. Freedom of conscience, freedom of the exchange of information, freedom of movement and of choice for one's country of residence are all inseparable from the goals of assuring international security, facilitating economic and social progress, and preserving our environment.[1]

THE JACKSON STAFF

Our political system, in its marvelous Madisonian confusion, requires energetic individual effort to achieve sound policy and effective political action. As a practical politician, Jackson was able to build up in his own Senate office a group of people of considerable political skill and, simultaneously, establish a network of citizen groups to provide "outside" support for his human rights initiatives.

The office staff was diverse in background and, to appearances, different from the Senator himself. Dr. Dorothy Fosdick, his principal foreign policy aide for over 28 years, was a seemingly improbable choice. Daughter of a prominent churchman, educated in the Ivy League, she had come to work in the State Department during World War II. In so doing, she had rejected the pacifism and isolation of many in her cohort. Richard Perle represented a similar anomaly in the next generation. Perle's father was a first generation American who migrated from New York to Los Angeles. In the 1960s, Perle studied at the University of Southern California and at Princeton, seemingly on his way to a career typical of the "bright young man" interested in international affairs. But Perle also parted company from his cohort. In the mid-1960s, the old establishment and the juniors who aspired to membership in it had already meandered into their collective nervous breakdown, reminiscent of the 1930s in Britain. Senator Jackson, however, held onto the old ground, and like a great force of political gravity, he pulled to him people of similar sentiment, though widely differing backgrounds that cut across the usual lines. Fosdick and Perle represented this, as did Tina Silber and Catherine Hill, two other members of the staff who were to play large roles in the human rights efforts. Silber, who had studied at Goucher College and the University of Pennsylvania in the 1960s, came to the Senator's staff from the American-Israel Public Affairs Committee. She was to be instrumental in extending support for the Jackson amendment to almost all parts of the American public with historical, religious, and cultural ties to the captive peoples under Soviet domination. Hill, on the other hand, belonged to Dr. Fosdick's cohort. She had had a varied career with much international experience. A lady of great common sense and easy dignity, she was an improbable choice to become the Senator's principal contact with various Americans of East European background, but that is what she did.

These people shared with Jackson a body of convictions and a capacity for old-fashioned moral judgment which transcended the style of the times. Indeed, in retrospect, it is this willingness to live on the wrong side of the "kulturkampf" which distinguished the Jackson organization from most of the rest of the political community that "mattered." He and his people were somehow resistant to all of the usual blandishments; successive administrations, Republican and Democratic, were just plain exasperated by it.

THE JACKSON AMENDMENT
ON FREEDOM OF EMIGRATION

Henry Jackson was, preeminently, a legislator. Almost by instinct, he had a sense for the organization of political action around a piece of legislation. The Jackson amendment, which linked certain American trade benefits to nonmarket countries to their respect for the right to emigrate, has become synomomous with a certain part of the international human rights movement in the 1970s. It drew its inspiration from the Universal Declaration of Human Rights, specifically Article XIII—"the right of everyone to leave any country, including his own, and to return to his country." The amendment was occasioned, really, by a resurgent self-regard among Jews in the Soviet Union following Israel's victory in the 1967 Six-Day War. This led to internal pressures for emigration to Israel, and the Soviet government responded by slowly increasing the number of Jews who were allowed to leave.

In 1972, however, the Soviet government imposed an infamous "education tax," nominally designed to compensate the state for the cost of higher education but, in reality, a way of curtailing and ultimately deterring any emigration efforts. At about the same time, the Nixon administration sought legislation which would make the Soviet Union eligible for most-favored-nation tariff treatment; it would also need legislative authority to increase subsidized lending to the Soviets. This interest in subsidized trade and credits for the Soviet Union reflected the Nixon-Kissinger theory that American economic aid would moderate Soviet international behavior.

Jackson seized an opportunity by introducing legislation that allowed the granting of these American concessions to nonmarket countries only if they showed respect for the right of their citizens to emigrate. The amendment did not affect normal trade on a pay-as-you go basis. And it applied to Jews, Christians, and others, without discrimination on the basis of race, religion or national origin.

The introduction of the Jackson amendment began a two-year legislative struggle. The Soviets and their allies within the American business community—and within the administration—did what they could to frustrate its passage. But in late 1974 it was, in modified form, passed into law.[2] The changes resulted from an intensive triangular negotiation involving Secretary of State Kissinger on behalf of the administration, the Soviets, and the Senator.

What resulted was a Soviet commitment for liberalized emigration in exchange for the granting and continuation of the trade benefits on an annual basis. In late December 1974, the Soviets decided to deny publicly that they had ever agreed to any of this; a decade later, they still remain ineligible for American trade concessions and special subsidies unless the President first certifies that they have provided the requisite assurances required by the amendment to permit freer emigration in the future.

The Jackson amendment has thus shown itself more than the expression of a piety; an issue of human rights has been written into a law with real consequences. Romania, Hungary and China have accepted the terms of the amendment. Tens of thousands who felt obliged to leave their homelands have successfully emigrated due in no small part to the amendment. It is still there, the law of the land, and remains the basis for any future bargaining between the United States and the Soviet Union on these issues.

A two-year struggle for the enactment of a piece of legislation can become a story of almost infinite complexity and one can extract from it any number of "meanings" and "interpretations." One felt, however, that it was the extraordinary collection of people who were touched by the Jackson amendment in one way or another that Jackson himself regarded as *the* most impressive thing. It was really quite remarkable. People and values and interests not always given political prominence somehow managed to gain an upper hand. Minority peoples of the Soviet Union, traditionally the most oppressed, contributed political inspiration. Jews and Ukrainians and Tartars and Baltic Peoples and Armenians and others; Baptists, Russian Orthodox, Roman Catholics, secular liberals; all seemed willing to defy the Soviet police state at enormous risk.

Of special significance to Jackson was an extraordinary "open letter" written by Andrei Sakharov and addressed to the Congress of the United States on September 14, 1973.[3] Sakharov urged adoption of the amendment as an essential first step marking the proper direction for the development of detente. According to him, the Soviet Union has for decades developed "under conditions of an intolerable isolation, bringing with it the ugliest consequences," and "even a partial preservation of those conditions would be highly perilous for all mankind, for international confidence and detente."

To wear away at this isolation, Sakharov wrote, the Soviets must accept basic international principles of conduct, among them respect for the right to emigrate as proclaimed in 1948 in the Universal Declaration of Human Rights. "The amendment," he stated, "does not represent interference in the internal affairs of socialist countries, but simply a defense of international law, without which there can be no mutual trust."

Sakharov emphasized that the technique of "quiet diplomacy" could not help anyone, "beyond a few individuals in Moscow and some other cities. . . . The abandonment of a policy of principle would be a betrayal of the thousands of Jews and non-Jews who want to emigrate, of the hundreds in camps and mental hospitals, of the victims of the Berlin Wall."

Whatever the political pressures in the United States, one could only feel ashamed if he contemplated abandoning a struggle for which those behind the Iron Curtain were prepared to risk all. All the sacrifices *were* "asymmetrical." Human rights activists in the Soviet Union—determined to keep the cause energized—were harassed, tortured, banished to internal exile, imprisoned. The worst one had to endure here was either the irate telephone call from the paid lobbyist of a corporation eager to get rich in the Soviet trade, or the more soothing entreaty from a Cabinet officer with a mellifluous voice and bogus *bonhomie*. The Jackson amendment was an exercise in populist foreign policy, a policy pushed forward by ordinary and humble American citizens in the face of bitter opposition. One gathered that, for Henry Jackson, its passage was a confirmation of his deepest instincts about people and democratic politics.

And, of course, for Jackson and his staff, there were occasions of very special celebration when brave individuals whom the Senator had personally championed finally made it to freedom—Simas Kudirka, Pastor Georgi Vins, Valery and Galina Panov, the Leonid Tarassuks, Vladimir Bukovsky, Alexander Galich, Andrei Amalrik, Vitali Rubin, Alexander Ginzburg, Valentin Moroz, Eduard Kuznetsov, the Chudnovsky family, Sylva Zalmanson, Mark Abramovich, Mstislav Rostropovich, Huber Matos and so many others.

The real and symbolic power of Jackson's amendment is in no way better confirmed than by the controversy that still surrounds it—more than a dozen years after its passage. Today, the President is not able to confer certain trade benefits on the Soviet Union, for he cannot assert that the Soviets are prepared to live up to the kind of commitments for freer emigration they conveyed in 1974. Soviet assurances, then, were passed along in the form of an October 18 letter from Secretary of State Kissinger to Jackson[4] and later, on December 3, 1974 in the form of testimony by the Secretary before the Senate Finance Committee.[5] But in late 1974, the Soviet government publicly disassociated itself from the undertakings Secretary Kissinger ascribed to it. That, in the formal sense, is where the matter *still* stands.

Predictably, the Soviets' decision to scrap the 1972 trade agreement and to repudiate the assurances on emigration they were said by Kissinger to have provided in 1974 became part of an ongoing argument. Opponents of Jackson's approach seized upon those events as a vindication of a minimalist approach—otherwise known as "quiet diplomacy." Subsequent declines in emigration from the Soviet Union were invoked as evidence that the Soviets did not respond to "pressure." Then, too, there was the claim that Jackson's initiative was designed to "wreck detente."

What is missing from arguments of this sort is a sense of scale and of history. The human rights movement inside the Soviet Union grew in scope because of its own efforts and of the outside support it received. The Soviet government, for its part, could be expected to do the minimum necessary in the field of human rights to advance its other objectives. The Jackson amendment set—and still sets—a higher standard of Soviet performance on the right to emigrate. Its success was, and still is, measured in the hundreds of thousands who have gained freedom under its general aegis and in the many who continue to emigrate from nonmarket countries that have accepted the terms of the amendment. Naturally, one welcomes the release of a handful of prominent Soviet human rights activists now and again. But when their arrival in the West is greeted as a victory for "quiet diplomacy," or as a sign of "new flexibility" we should understand not that Jackson's demarche failed, but that contemporary standards of success have shrunk to almost nothing. Indeed, one suspects that this is what the minimalist "quiet diplomacy" approach is really all about—an effort to condition Western publics into accepting a lower standard of Soviet human rights performance, rather than encouraging Western publics to persevere in demanding high standards as the condition of "improved relations" between East and West.

As for the innuendo that the Jackson amendment was a ploy to wreck "detente," it should now be abundantly clear that the collapse of the so-called "detente" of the 70s had other more profound causes—including the Kremlin's geopolitical designs and activities. Jackson certainly believed that any genuine detente had to be based on a real accommodation as evidenced by a greater Soviet respect for human rights. But it was hardly Jackson's insistence on this fundamental point which brought "detente" to grief. The Jackson amendment was modest legislation of unusual influence, but one can scarcely ascribe to it the Middle East War of 1973, the violation of the 1973 Indochina peace accords, the Soviet-Cuban invasion of Angola, Vietnam's invasion of Cambodia, the Soviet invasion of Afghanistan—not to mention assorted Soviet violations of strategic arms agreements.

Even more, there is still much to be said for Jackson's emphasis on the tangible and the human. Like Solzhenitsyn in 1975, Anatoly Shcharansky came to the Capitol in 1986. "No amount of bargaining," he said, "of give and take, of mutual concessions, can take the place of trust. Experience has taught the Jews of the Soviet Union, has taught me while I was in the camps struggling against the KGB, that lesser demands and fewer expectations lead to a situation where our aggressors feel that they should be rewarded for cosmetic concessions." He therefore urged the Congress to "maintain and reinforce" the Jackson-Vanik amendment.[6]

THE CONTINUING JACKSON CONTRIBUTION

For all the human intensity surrounding the Jackson amendment, for all the thousands of lives bettered by it, and for all the affection Jackson's colleagues and aides now feel for that stimulative time, it is still wrong to think of that as his principal contribution to the enhancement of human rights. Far more important: he taught a generation how to think about the problems and dilemmas in this area, and provided more than one instance of political courage in coping with them.

Interestingly, when asked once what he regarded as his single most important accomplishment, the Senator said it was when in 1960 as Democratic National Chairman for John F. Kennedy's successful Presidential campaign, "We put an end to religious bigotry as a major factor in American politics."[7]

Scoop saw the human rights implication of the Vietnam War, and understood that the defeat of the United States would undermine the forces of law and civilization in the most fundamental way. Among Democrats in the Senate, he was almost alone in resisting irresponsible and dangerous—and often disingenuous proposals—to end the American involvement without proper regard for the consequences. About this, he was tragically correct, for we know now that the Indochina War was a human rights issue of almost unprecedented dimensions. The plight of the "boat people," the massacres in Cambodia, and all the other attendant brutalities of despotic rule place Indochina—along with Stalin's purges and the Holocaust itself—among the most grim events of this century.

For all this, Jackson's response to the collapse of South
Vietnam in April 1975 was predictable. One doubts that he
was surprised by the adversary's massive violations of the
1973 peace agreements or by the role of the Soviets in
underwriting the final North Vietnam invasion. Yet, in the
midst of the crisis, his office once again became a focus of
international rescue. It happened that the late Edward
Daly, President of World Airways, decided to organize an
airlift of Vietnamese children out of the country, and
Jackson played a helpful—but quiet and almost unno-
ticed—role in making that possible.

We remember that period as one of national exhaustion
and enormous self-doubt. In fact, the late 1970s was a most
difficult period for keeping the politics of foreign affairs on
a stable and sensible course. The American defeat in Indochina was followed by an ideological and geopolitical offensive by the Soviets. It was the time when they established
themselves in Ethiopia, Angola, and Aden, and when totalitarian and anti-Semitic forces made their largest gains in
"world opinion" in general and at the United Nations in
particular. These were followed by the Soviet invasion of
Afghanistan, which has since produced death and displace-
ment of historic dimensions. Afghanistan will soon super-
sede Cambodia as the most devastated country of our time.
Here, then, were conspicuous failures at a United States
"human rights" policy, and it was not obvious how they
might be retrieved.

The emphasis that President Carter placed on human
rights in international affairs failed to have the desired
effect; what purported to be a policy of conviction and
strength turned out to be a reaffirmation of weakness.
The Carter policy reduced to American pressure on the
weak states of the world that had some degree of depen-

dence on the United States. In was noteworthy for its unwillingness to take on the powerful and, therefore, the most dangerous human rights violators.

Jackson considered this approach fundamentally unwise, and he challenged President Carter to do better. As he put it in an April 24, 1980 dinner speech honoring Andrei Sakharov:

> I know that many here tonight share my continuing dismay at an American policy on human rights that finds it convenient to criticize petty dictatorships, with which the world unhappily abounds, but inconvenient to speak out about the Soviet system which inspires repression around the world. . . . For too many officials, the intensity of the struggle for human rights abroad is inversely proportional to the power of the offender. . . . Only with sensible priorities can we hope to forge an effective policy out of the impulse to support the cause of international human rights. Only by reasserting our concern at the denial of basic rights in the Soviet Union can we make credible our concern about basic rights elsewhere.[8]

Jackson's point of view retained considerable force inside the first Reagan administration. The President in the first instance had a marked affinity for Democrats of the Henry Jackson stripe, and several of them were appointed to significant positions. The Reagan administration sought to restore the proper balance between the humanitarian *and* the political aspects of a human rights policy; the President himself was democracy's most forceful advocate, confident that our political philosophy was on the move in the world.

Analysts will argue about who deserves what share of the credit for the worldwide movement toward democracy these past five years. But there is no denying the startling shift from military regimes to elected governments throughout Latin America, or the restoration of civilian rule in Turkey, or the growing respect for free societies and free enterprise on every continent. In 1975, Daniel P. Moynihan, soon to take up his responsibilities as our embattled representative at the United Nations, could wonder whether democracy in the twentieth century had come to resemble monarchy in the nineteenth—a system on the way out of history. A decade later, one hardly hears such a grim prognosis for us. Can anyone deny that at least some of the credit belongs to Senator Jackson, who kept alive the best in our internationalist tradition when it was demanding and discouraging to do so? Indeed it is a mark of Jackson's standing that the ideas associated with him have an enduring influence, that they have grown in their political relevance even after his death. Separated from that extraordinary base of parliamentary power which he built up across four decades, his ideas still retain an independent power of their own.

On June 26, 1984, dozens of Senator Jackson's friends and admirers met in the Rose Garden, adjacent to the Oval Office. Jackson himself had twice sought the Presidency, which added a particular poignancy to the gathering. President Reagan made a posthumous presentation of the Medal of Freedom, the nation's highest civilian commendation, to the Senator. In his remarks, the President touched on the great range of Jackson's contributions, but it was to the simple theme of human freedom that he returned at the end. "For those who make freedom their cause," the President said, "Henry Jackson will always inspire honor, courage, and hope."[9]

Senator Jackson and the
U.S. Relationship with Israel

BERNARD LEWIS

Bernard Lewis was Cleveland E. Dodge Professor of Near Eastern Studies and Long-Term Member of the Institute for Advanced Study, Princeton, New Jersey from 1974–86.

He first met Senator Jackson in March 1971 when he was invited to testify before the Jackson Subcommittee, and he and the Senator subsequently kept in touch informally on Near Eastern issues.

From 1949–74 he was Professor of the History of the Near and Middle East, School of Oriental and African Studies, London. He is author, co-author or editor of over twenty books on the history and contemporary problems of Islam and the Middle East, including *The Arabs in History* 1950 (ten times reprinted) and *The Middle East and the West* 1964. BA 1936 and PhD 1939 University of London.

Ⅰn March 1971, Senator Jackson asked me to come to Washington and testify before his Subcommittee on National Security and International Operations, and to give my views on the current situation in the Middle East. I was a trifle alarmed by the word "testify," the precise local connotation of which I did not at that time recognize. But I was anxious to seize the opportunity to make the personal acquaintance of a man whose words and actions I had long admired from afar. I therefore managed to overcome these and some other misgivings. It was the beginning of a long association, which lasted until his untimely death.

In the course of our association, I got to know him better and, in consequence, to respect him more. In particular, I was able to achieve some understanding of certain features of his public life—his principles and his concerns—which had surprised, and at times indeed perplexed, many observers unfamiliar with the man.

One of the abiding concerns of Henry M. Jackson's political life was his commitment to the survival and well-being of the State of Israel and to the fostering and development of the U.S. relationship with that country. In countries where ethnic and confessional loyalties tend to take precedence of all others, so deep and lasting a commitment in one who was not himself Jewish often caused wonderment. In circles where political and more specifically electoral expediency often influences and sometimes determines policy, such a choice, in a Senator whose political career was as representative of a state with a minute Jewish population, was also a source of surprise.

ROOTS OF THE SENATOR'S CONCERN
AND SUPPORT FOR ISRAEL

Jackson himself, when questioned on this matter, dated his interest in the Jewish national home and later the State of Israel from that day in 1945 when, two days after its liberation by the United States Army, he entered the German concentration camp at Buchenwald and saw for himself the awful consequences of prejudice, hatred, and the actions to which they led. Always a close observer of the East European scene, Jackson soon realized that for the shattered remnants of East European Jewry there was no hope, no hope at all, of rebuilding their lives in the countries from which they had come. The roots of hatred were too deep, the seeds too far-flung—and the new regimes that were being established showed no disposition to remove, preferring rather to exploit, the ancient hatreds. The great countries of immigration in the new world and elsewhere were still in the main closed to refugees, and where the strict rules were relaxed it was not usually the victims of persecution that were welcomed. Like many other observers of the time, both Jews and non-Jews, Senator Jackson came to the conclusion that only in the Jewish national home arising in Palestine could the shattered remnants of continental European Jewry hope to find new homes and rebuild a new life.

Sadly, the problem of Jewish persecution did not end with the emptying of the camps in Europe. In the wake of the European Jews came great numbers of Jews from Arab countries, where the ancient Jewish communities established there were subjected to new pressures and new waves of persecution. When they too had been accommodated in the national home, now transformed into a sovereign state, there were the Soviet Jews, whose hopes for freedom aroused the Senator's compassion and concern.

A humanitarian concern for the victims of persecution may have been the beginning of Jackson's interest in Jewish refugees and of the new state that was created to receive them. His continued support of the State of Israel during more than 30 years of its checkered political existence sprang, however, from other considerations of a more directly political, and in a sense also an ideological character. Ultimately, Scoop's support for Israel was an expression of the two basic concerns that dominated his political life—a passionate belief in liberal democracy and of the civilized human values which it enshrines, together with a keen awareness of the external threat to the democracies and to these values, and of the need for effective action in their defense.

For Scoop, commitment to a cause was not limited to holding certain beliefs and from time to time expressing them in words. He was quick to see the need for action, and to devise and undertake the kind of action that was required. Time and again, when something had to be done to defend or apply the policies in which he believed, it was the Senator who assembled, organized and led the coalitions that put these policies into effect.

EMPHASIS ON ISRAELI-EGYPTIAN COOPERATION

As a friend of Israel, Scoop Jackson was very far from being an enemy of the Arabs. On the contrary, there were numerous occasions in which he expressed deep compassion for the poverty and instability which plague most Middle Eastern countries, and for all the terrible human problems to which they give rise. From the first, he saw the importance of the Sadat peace initiative, and of the immense benefits which it could bring, not the least to the people of Egypt and of other countries in the region. In a speech delivered in 1978, he spoke in moving terms of the new opportunities created by the Camp David agreements:

At this time the Camp David agreements remain a political framework—a foundation—for the construction of a new political relationship between Israel and Egypt.

The Middle East, with the exception of Israel, and despite vast oil revenues, remains plagued by poverty and instability. While a four-fold increase in the price of oil has enriched a small minority in a few countries, the great mass in the Middle East continue to suffer the burdens of inadequate food and shelter, high unemployment and a dismal future. A major factor in the tensions that have produced a generation of political instability in the Middle East has been the desperation that afflicts all but a handful of rich and privileged individuals.

For example, the Egyptian people, some 38 million and growing by over a million each year, live from hand to mouth. In Cairo, where six million people are crowded together, the ancient cemetery area—the city of the dead—has become a city of the near living, where hundreds of thousands of urban poor live, without water, plumbing or electricity, inside tombs.

Ten percent of the infants born each year die in infancy. Many of the survivors are afflicted by trachoma and otitis media, disabling eye and hearing diseases.

In the Upper Nile, and in farming areas generally, schistosomiasis is virtually universal—a parasitic disease that contributes to Egypt's male life expectancy of 54 years and condemns millions to internal bleeding, debilitation and suffering. Professionals and skilled workers emigrate in droves—for there is no work for them in Egypt.

This can and must be changed. The potential resources are rich and plentiful. With peace they can be developed, and with peace one can imagine a fruitful partnership of unprecedented proportions between Israel, Egypt and the United States.

In helping to alleviate poverty in Egypt and elsewhere in the Middle East, I believe that there is a great and historic role for the United States, a role that we once before were able to play in the reconstruction of postwar Europe.

As was the case with the Marshall Plan, it is essential that any such program for the Middle East be based on a full partnership with the Israelis and Egyptians. They should work with us for the common development of their countries and, eventually, the region as a whole. Among them, the countries possess all the potential resources: capital, ingenuity, management skills, labor and, with our involvement, technology and markets. Together we can do much to reverse the misery of centuries, to make the deserts bloom. . . .

The American government can and should let all the countries of the Middle East know that there is a path to the realization of their peaceful dreams along which we are willing to accompany them. And at the same time we must make it plain that those who are unwilling to join with us and Israel and Egypt will lose out on the economic and other benefits of cooperation and mutual assistance. . . .

The Camp David Agreements are, we trust, a significant step on the road to a stable peace in the Middle East. At the end of that road there are enormous, and enormously positive possibilities—that all the people of the region will discover the truth about their neighbors as the walls that have divided them for so long come down. For the peace to last it must be more than a peace among armies and diplomats, more than an official peace. It must come to occupy a place in the daily lives of Arabs and Israelis alike. There must be movement across once fortified borders that can now become gateways to the development of social and political and economic relations—first among the Israeli and

Egyptian people, and in time among all those in the Arab world
who are willing to live in peace.[1]

COMPASSION AND STRENGTH:
COMPLEMENTARY POLICIES

To many of the postwar generation, born and reared in
peace and safety and schooled in innocence, for whom
fascism means heavy-handed policemen and no more,
there appeared to be a paradox, even a contradiction,
between Scoop Jackson's liberal and compassionate positions on domestic matters and his strong positions on
foreign policy and defense. For those of us who belong to
an older generation—those of us who recall fascism when
it was a terrible reality and not just a loosely used term of
abuse, who encountered Hitler in a major war in which
the issue was our survival and the outcome was long in
doubt, there was no contradiction between the two policies, which were on the contrary complementary. The
Senator knew very well that the threat to our civilization
did not end with the defeat of the Axis; that a new threat
had arisen and was rapidly developing against which vigilance and action were needed to defend not just our
country, but the civilization of which it has become the
leader and the champion, and the human values which it
embodies. And, since the threat is world-wide, so too must
be the defense, and this in turn imposes the need to seek
out and to sustain reliable allies.

WHAT MAKES A RELIABLE ALLY?

But what is an ally? Unlike too many politicians, Jackson
knew that an alliance, if it is to have any value and any

permanence, must rest on more than a strategic and/or political alignment with a government, which might itself be fragile and with which any alliance is of necessity temporary, lasting only as long as the ruler stays in power and does not change his mind. In autocratic states, and, unfortunately, most of the states in the world today are autocracies of one kind or another, the sudden death or ouster of the ruler—or even some new whim of the ruler who remains in power—can bring a total realignment. The moment of uncertainty following the murder of King Faisal in Saudi Arabia, the changes in Libya following the deposition of King Idris, illustrate on the one hand the danger, on the other the reality of change.

A real alliance must depend on more than a temporary accommodation in political alignment or choice of policies by incumbent leaders. It must rest on a real affinity—on a deep and authentic community of tradition, of institutions, of aspirations, and ultimately on a shared way of life. Such is the nature of our alliances with the democracies of Western Europe and Australasia. Such too is the relationship with Israel. A relationship of this kind will survive any change of policy or leadership because a pro-Western and hence pro-American policy in such a country is structural—it is part of the very nature of their society and their culture, and whatever disagreements may occur on specific questions, for such a society to become hostile to the United States is virtually impossible. To achieve this result, the society itself would have to be changed.

The Soviets have well understood this principle—hence their determination, when they have power or even when they have influence, to create Soviet-style dictatorships in their own image. Such has been the fate of South Yemen and Ethiopia, of some of the states of Southeast Asia, and of others in Central America. Such is not yet the fate of Afghanistan.

ISRAEL'S ACHIEVEMENTS AS A DEMOCRACY

It is not always easy to create a Soviet-style, Marxist dictatorship in Asian and African countries. It is infinitely more difficult to create a Western-style democracy. Such a polity cannot be imported, still less imposed. It can only be nurtured and grown by the people of the country, drawing on their own history, their own traditions and laws, their own culture. Sometimes such democracies emerge or re-emerge, in toil and anguish, after hard struggles, either out of defeat, as in postwar Germany, Italy, and Japan, or from internal sources, as more recently in Spain and the Argentine. Sometimes the struggle is still continuing, as in Greece and Turkey. Sometimes it begins and is nipped in the bud, as in Hungary and Poland. But nowhere has it been imposed, and there are few places where it flourishes outside its homelands in Western Europe and the countries colonized by West Europeans overseas.

There are indeed few such places and one of them is Israel where despite 38 years of a continuing state of war and the inevitable stress on the military, no military regime has emerged; where despite continuing security censorship, freedom of the press and of public debate is flourishing; where despite ruinous economic burdens, the open society still works; where despite enormous diversity and internal as well as external strains, a thriving, lively, highly self-critical democracy is as active as ever.

Scoop Jackson was able to see and appreciate this achievement. He knew its value both in itself, and as a bastion not merely of American interests but in a deeper sense of the standards and values for which the United States has stood and now more than ever still stands in the world. To those who saw Israel as an incubus, as an imped-iment to what might otherwise be a successful United States policy in the Middle East, he asked how well we had done in other regions where there is no Israel—such as Central America, Southern Africa, and Southeast Asia. The answers, and the lessons, are clear.

The China Policy of
Henry Jackson

MICHEL OKSENBERG AND DWIGHT H. PERKINS

Michel Oksenberg is Professor of Political Science and Research Associate of the Center for Chinese Studies at The University of Michigan. He was the second Henry M. Jackson Visiting Professor of Modern Chinese Studies at the Henry M. Jackson School of International Studies.

He first met with Senator Jackson in 1973, informally consulting with him from time to time thereafter. From 1977 to 1980, as staff member of the National Security Council, with special responsibility for China and the Indochina states, he and Senator Jackson were in frequent communication. He accompanied the Senator as adviser on his last trip to the People's Republic of China in August 1983.

He has authored, co-authored, or edited a number of books on China and is a regular contributor to journals and symposium volumes dealing with the PRC and other Asian nations. BA 1960 Swarthmore College; MA 1963 and PhD 1969 Columbia University.

Dwight H. Perkins has been Director of the Harvard Institute for International Development since 1980, and is concurrently Professor of Political Economy in the Department of Economics, Harvard University, and Member of the Harvard Faculty of Arts and Sciences and the Kennedy School of Government. He was the first Henry M. Jackson Visiting Professor of Modern Chinese Studies at the Henry M. Jackson School of International Studies.

In July 1974 he accompanied Senator Jackson as adviser on the Senator's first official trip to the People's Republic of China. Thereafter, he was in frequent touch with the Senator, joining him on his second and third China visits in February 1978 and August 1979.

He is the author, co-author, or editor of nine books and many articles, mostly dealing with the economic development of China, Korea and other parts of Asia. BA 1956 Cornell University; MA 1961 and PhD 1964 Harvard University.

The Manchurian passenger express lurched from Harbin to Dalian on a hot August night in 1983. In a pullman compartment, Henry Jackson enthralled his companions as he recalled the Senators whom he most admired in the course of his distinguished career. Someone had asked Senator Jackson to list the ten Senators, past and present, whom he most respected. The conversation began with four people in the compartment. Gradually, more and more in the Senator's travelling party joined, until the latecomers were standing at the door, straining to hear the Senator's words above the clickity-clack punctuating the train's progress in the night. All recognized that something special was occurring: we were sharing in history in a most intimate, relaxed, and powerful form.

Within ten days, Senator Jackson was dead. The evening lives in the memories of its participants, for Senator Jackson had given the key to knowing him. Neither the Senator's China policy, nor his approach to other great national issues which captured his interest, can be understood without recognizing the qualities he valued in public officials.

The Senator whom Jackson first recalled was Richard Russell of Georgia. He understood the need for military preparedness; he had a sense of history and strategy. Here was a man of honor, integrity and principle. Then came Paul Douglas of Illinois, closer to Senator Jackson than Russell in terms of commitment to the pursuit of justice at home. Douglas was a classic civil libertarian, courageous,

143

wed to Jackson in both their contempt for McCarthyism and their strong anti-communism. Scoop then said he had to mention Sam Rayburn of Texas. Rayburn had befriended Jackson, as the Speaker did so many other freshmen, when Jackson first entered the House of Representatives. Rayburn knew no peer in his understanding of and respect for the parliamentary institutions in which he worked. He too was a man of honor. His word and a handshake meant a commitment had been made.

Senator Mansfield of Montana was also high on Jackson's list for his integrity, balance, and competence. As Senator and Ambassador to Japan, Mansfield had evidenced a sense of history, especially of American policy in East Asia, which Jackson admired. Jackson did not always agree with him, differing with Mansfield's frequent calls for a unilateral reduction in the American forces in Europe. John Stennis of Mississippi, his colleague on the Senate Armed Services Committee, was a long-time, key ally in emphasizing military preparedness. Stennis and Mansfield, the Senator stressed, were both astute politicians and principled individuals.

Jackson praised, among others, Clinton Anderson, Walter George, John Pastore, Herbert Lehman, and John McClellan. Strikingly, all those Jackson mentioned were Democrats. He partook of the traditions of his party to a deeper extent than perhaps many observers understood. But, all were Democrats of a particular stripe: those who clearly put their nation ahead of their party. Particularly during the Republican administrations of Eisenhower, Nixon, and Ford, Jackson's Democrats sought to forge a bipartisan foreign policy and to rally behind the President in moments when they perceived that important national security issues were at stake.

None who left the Senator's pullman seminar that August night had any doubt. Henry Jackson was a proud lion. He considered himself a guardian of his beloved institution. He was worried about its future; he felt that, for many reasons, the Senate was experiencing great change, and perhaps too few in the chamber embodied the qualities that had elicited his respect: honor, patriotism, integrity, vision, mastery of detail, effectiveness, steadfastness in purpose.

At the time of his Manchurian pullman seminar, Senator Jackson was a national spokesman on China policy. He was known as a leading Senate authority on China and a strong proponent of expanded Sino-American ties. He had exerted a major influence on American relations with China and was at the very center of policy-making on the key issues. His desire to enhance further his understanding of China and to follow up on earlier discussions with Chinese leaders had prompted him to undertake the arduous journey—his fourth official visit to China since 1974.

JACKSON ON CHINA: BACKGROUND

Senator Jackson's public participation in reappraising American policy toward China began in early 1966. Exactly what combination of events prompted his decision to add this issue to his agenda is not altogether clear, but a number of factors certainly contributed.[1]

For one thing, the Senator did not want to waste his time on quixotic ventures. He was interested in getting positive results where he judged they were politically possible. Before moving on an issue he characteristically estimated its ripeness: could it be constructively advanced and would his own involvement make a difference?

During the 1950s and 60s Jackson was already fully occupied with an agenda of domestic, defense, and international issues where he saw opportunities to advance national policy. Moreover, those were the years of political convulsions within China leading into the terror and political repressions of the Cultural Revolution, the Korean and Vietnam conflicts in which China, under Mao, was in an adversarial role, and the ascendancy of the Taiwan lobby in American politics (especially in the Senate). Obviously, the opportunities to improve significantly Chinese-American relations were not auspicious.

Nevertheless, Jackson's interest in China had long been there. Early in his life he came to appreciate the talents of the Chinese people and noted the capacity of the Chinese to endure great hardship. He had always spoken with deep respect for China's historic contribution to human civilization. Born and bred on the Pacific rim, and given his geopolitical perspective on the world, it is not surprising that he never confused the island of Taiwan with China proper, the potential Pacific and global great power comprising almost one-fourth of mankind. In fact, through all the vicissitudes of the so-called McCarthy era and the political sway of the pro-Taiwan elements, Jackson studiously kept his distance from the Taiwan lobby and from associations with Chiang Kai-shek.

Interestingly, Senator Jackson used his position as Chairman of the Subcommittee on National Policy Machinery of the Committee on Government Operations to sponsor research on the Chinese political system. In 1960, the Subcommittee published *National Policy Machinery in Communist China*.[2] At a time when very little information existed on how the Chinese system worked, this objective and incisive thirty-page study was very useful. The study became required reading in many courses on China within the government and on campuses. It reflected Jackson's appreciation of the need for improved understanding of contemporary China.

By 1963 Senator Jackson had begun to think hard about the Sino-Soviet dispute and its effect on America's security position and choices. He apparently recognized this issue well before it received extensive attention within the Washington national security community. His public comments indicate an awareness not only of the ideological component of the struggle, but also of the historic nationalistic distrust between Russians and Chinese, as well as the competitive striving for power between the leadership of the two countries, notably Khrushchev and Mao. He had begun to identify the route through which a change in U.S.-China relations could be effected.

Clearly, the Vietnam War contributed to concentrating Jackson's attention on U.S. relations with China. Jackson had initially thought that China was the major culprit. His analysis of the conflict had been heavily influenced by repeated U.S. government intelligence briefings that Vietnam's principal backer was China and that China would be the principal great power beneficiary of a communist victory. But as the war unfolded Jackson came to realize that American intelligence on China and on the implications of the Sino-Soviet dispute was mistaken and that Hanoi's interests coincided more with Moscow than with Beijing. This became for Jackson a casebook example of how U.S. government intelligence can suffer a massive failure.

By 1966 the Senator was evidently moving toward the conclusion that China was not the major transgressor or beneficiary of the Vietnam War and that settling the conflict on honorable, negotiable terms and improving relations with China were separable issues and that the time had come to call for a new approach to China policy.

JACKSON ON CHINA, 1966–1971: SEIZING THE ISSUE

In March 1966 Senator Fulbright's Foreign Relations Committee held notable hearings on China, and in May, Senator Kennedy and Senator McGovern gave major addresses urging reappraisal of American policy toward China. They reached their position, in part, as critics of the Vietnam War. But—still publicly supporting the administration in its Vietnam efforts—Jackson joined the discussion on the Senate floor to indicate his interest in getting the problem of relations with China before the American people:

> I wish to take this opportunity to commend the distinguished junior Senator from Massachusetts for bringing this issue out into the open once again and getting it into the mainstream of American thought and concern. I do not know of anything more important than to get this issue properly before the public.[3]

A month later, in a commencement address at Whitman College, Senator Jackson described the five major new issues which would challenge American foreign policy in the coming decades.[4] One of these was "working out, in the years ahead, a livable relationship with the Chinese communists." Jackson noted that "Peking had shown a certain respect for the very great strength the United States has maintained in the Pacific area since the Korean War." Turning to the implications of the Sino-Soviet dispute, Jackson continued, "Russia and China have come pute, Jackson continued, "Russia and China have come close to the breaking point, and it is obvious that their relations will not be what they have been—a fact of potentially enormous significance for China's role in world affairs."

In July, President Johnson gave a speech on Asia to the American Alumni Council in which he called for reconciliation with China, based on the twin notions that the United States is inescapably a Pacific power and that a peaceful China is essential to a peaceful Asia. The speech elicited praise in editorials from three newspapers: the *Baltimore Sun,* the *Philadelphia Inquirer,* and the *Washington Evening Star.* Jackson used the opportunity to enter these editorials into the *Congressional Record,* noting that, "Each comments with approval on his (i.e., Johnson's) call to Communist China for an atmosphere of conciliation."[5]

The major turning point for Jackson came in a speech to the Seattle Rotary Club on November 5, 1969. He said, in part:

I believe it would contribute to peace and stability in the Western Pacific if Communist China, comprising over seven hundred million people, could begin to re-enter the international community and place its international relations on a more normal, stable plane. . . . As far as United States policy toward Mainland China is concerned, I believe we should get it on a less-rigid, more sensible footing.

We should renew the invitation to the Peking regime to join in the 25-nation arms control meetings in Geneva. . . . We should press Peking for the reopening of the bilateral U.S.-China Ambassadorial talks . . . and be prepared to make constructive suggestions for discussion and negotiation. . . . These suggestions should include: the start of mutual U.S.-Chinese exchanges of reporters, scholars, scientists and cultural performers; the improvement of trade relations between U.S. and Mainland China, including the mutual reduction of barriers to trade; the subject of Mainland Chinese participation in the United Nations and other international bodies on terms that would not exclude the Republic of China on Formosa. . . . It is time that both the Americans and the Mainland Chinese recognized that they have a mutual interest in, and a mutual responsibility for, peace and stability in the Western Pacific area.[6]

This speech dates the Senator's full, public commitment to a constructive Sino-American relationship. The text suggests that certain immediate considerations affected the timing of his initiative. First, the Sino-Soviet military confrontation of early 1969, the danger of a Sino-Soviet war, and the resumption of Sino-Soviet talks had all attracted his attention. He sensed danger if we did not move forward. Second, he mentioned signs of possible Chinese interest in resuming the U.S.-PRC ambassadorial talks in Warsaw. He saw opportunity. Third, he reflected on the implications of China's rapidly developing nuclear program and the ultimate need to incorporate China into any effective arms control regimen. He saw the long-term desirability of a change in policy. Finally, the new Nixon administration had initiated the policy of Vietnamization, and American participation in the conflict was winding down. The Senator was free to focus on post-Vietnam Asia.

Jackson thus joined the advocates for an opening to China prior to the initiation of Sino-American "ping-pong" diplomacy in the spring of 1970 and before Kissinger's secret visit of July 1971. Even preceding his Rotary Club speech, he had instructed his staff to assemble a report on *Peking's Approach to Negotiations*.[7] And in May 1970, in response to an October 1969 instruction before the initiation of ping-pong diplomacy, his staff published a study in anticipation of Sino-American academic exchanges.[8]

By early 1971, Jackson had become a leading advocate of developing ties with China. Again his words merit quoting:

It is generally agreed that by one formula or another the way will be opened to Peking to be admitted to the United Nations if not this fall, then in the fall of 1972. Rather than concentrate U.S. efforts on how we can best delay such entry we should be thinking more as to how we may utilize the presence of the Mainland Chinese in the UN and of a delegation in New York to improve our relationship with Peking. . . .

It is obvious that sometime, somehow, the Mainland Chinese regime will have to join in the negotiations on arms control. No strategic arms control agreement with a loophole as large as China could survive Chinese acquisition of a substantial nuclear force. . . .

Our treaty obligations for the defense and security of the Republic of China on Taiwan will continue whatever the formula whereby Mainland China enters the UN. We have a long record of alliance and friendship with the Republic of China on Taiwan. We will continue this close association, and I do not believe it need constitute a block to the movement toward more normal relations between the U.S. and Mainland China.[9]

A year and a half ago I proposed that this country should get its policy toward Mainland China on a less-rigid, more sensible footing. We should press ahead and accomplish what we can to improve mutual relations with Peking. The resumption of the bilateral talks in Warsaw, the implementation of a variety of exchange programs, and a renewal of trade could be steps in the direction of normalizing our bilateral relations. The pursuit of such reciprocal activities might well form a basis for a restoration of diplomatic relations between the United States and the People's Republic of China.[10]

It is, of course, impossible to measure the influence of any single political figure, and one cannot fully assess the impact which Jackson's speeches, private initiatives, and other activities had from 1966 to 1971. But, the record is clear: he was consistently ahead of policy, he entered the national debate when the long-frozen issue had become fluid, and he helped articulate the new consensus.

CHINA SPECIALIST
AND NATIONAL SPOKESMAN, 1972–1983

The Nixon administration's opening to China and the winding down of the Vietnam War enabled Senator Jackson to become one of the Senate's leading specialists on China and to influence American policy toward China in positive fashion.

The energetic and methodical way he set upon his task reveals much about the man. Respectful of academic, business and government expertise, he developed a coterie of advisers whom he frequently consulted and from whom he sought ideas and information. He sought out the China specialists at the State Department, the Central Intelligence Agency, and the National Security Council, cultivating ties with those he found compatible, and he encouraged his staff—especially Dickie Fosdick—to assist those in the executive branch when problems arose on the Hill. He was ready to help the specialists at higher levels within the administration, if they felt their cause was becoming bogged down. By placing himself at the nexus of the private sector, administration and congressional interactions on China—even though he was not on the Foreign Relations Committee—he insured that he would be at the cutting edge of the issues in this area.

Jackson developed ties with the Liaison Office of the People's Republic of China when the Chinese established their presence in Washington in 1973, cultivating a warm personal relationship with the successive ambassadors. He knew what was on their mind and they knew of his concerns. They regularly called on him to talk over mutual problems and to get his help and advice in interpreting the American political scene and the import of current American policies. He made himself available to visiting Chinese delegations, making it a point to receive the ranking visitors. He understood the entrée that this would provide him in China. He used the ties he had established within the Carter administration and with the Chinese to persuade Deng Xiaoping, during his famous January–February 1979 trip, to visit Seattle where he then hosted the Chinese leader.

Jackson made four official trips to China, in 1974, 1978, 1979, and 1983. On each occasion, he held wide-ranging discussions on foreign and domestic affairs, including one-on-one conversations with Deng Xiaoping that dwelled at length on the most sensitive aspects of Sino-American relations and on the domestic situation in the two countries. As time progressed and Chinese trust in him grew, he served as an intermediary between the two countries. On his last trip, for example, he handcarried a letter from President Reagan to Chinese leaders and he assisted in establishing the sequence of visits in 1984 by Premier Zhao Ziyang to Washington and President Reagan to China.

Nor, on his trips to China, did he content himself with conversations in Beijing. He toured the country, visiting different regions as part of his effort to understand the cultural diversity, the history, the strategic issues, and the developmental problems China faced in building a modern nation. He traveled to areas bordering the Soviet Union—including the remote Xinjiang region, Inner Mongolia, and

Heilongjiang province in the northeast—as well as such core provinces in the east as Shandong, Jiangsu, and Shanghai.

In all these travels the Senator found himself welcomed as a VIP. Wherever he went large, friendly crowds gathered. True to form as the inveterate campaigner, Scoop worked the crowds—for example, shaking hands with hundreds of curious students who in 1974 surrounded him on a university campus in Soochow and on a freezing February day in 1978 smiling and waving through the Shengli oilfields in a way the staff predicted would have elected him to the Central Committee in a landslide.

The Senator admired the Chinese "sense of humor," and it evoked his own lighter side. Some guests barely survive the inevitable, elegant, thirteen-course banquets which are the Chinese mark of hospitality for VIPs, and are repeated one after another as one moves about China. But Scoop found the key to enjoyable survival. Between serious discussions, he led his hosts in story telling, playful banter, and spirited repartee. Everyone delighted in it.

In 1979 the Senator flew to Urumchi and then on to Ining on China's farthest northwestern border with the Soviet Union. From a border post commander, he heard about the maneuvers with live ammunition that Soviet troops had conducted a few miles away during China's war with Vietnam. In Huhehot in Inner Mongolia, he gained an appreciation of what the Chinese meant by people's war from a briefing on and visit to aspects of the militia defense system of the city. At one point in the visit, a garage door was opened and the delegation drove down into a defense tunnel not to emerge until eight kilometers later outside the city. Jackson's four trips were genuine study missions. Each culminated in a serious public report to the Senate.[11]

In this way, Jackson began to exert a subtle influence on American policy. He wrote timely personal letters to our recent Presidents and Secretaries of State when he sensed policy was going awry. He met in confidence on several occasions with Presidents Nixon, Ford, Carter, and Reagan to convey his understanding of the importance of China in our foreign policy. He played a significant role behind the scenes in such initiatives as recommending Dr. Zbigniew Brzezinski's pivotal May 1978 trip to China, encouraging Secretary of Energy James Schlesinger to visit in the fall of 1978 to promote cooperation in the energy sphere, securing the submission and congressional passage of the trade agreement with China in the fall of 1979 providing for the extension of most-favored-nation treatment and access to official credits, and encouraging the visits of Secretary of State George Shultz and Secretary of Defense Caspar Weinberger to China in 1983. His strong support for normalization had an effect on the way President Carter and his aides interwove their policies toward Beijing and Moscow, inducing added care in not allowing problems with the Soviets to delay forward movement with China. Jackson stood aloof from the debate over the Taiwan Relations Act, but he quietly let the administration know that he was prepared, if necessary, to enter the fray if the administration concluded that the wording of key passages ran counter to the Shanghai Communique.

THE STRATEGIC VIEW

What shared strategic perspective drew Jackson toward China and the Chinese leaders toward him? The Senator's position on relations with the Soviet Union had something to do with the first invitation to visit China as did the fact that Jackson was the one major Democratic Presidential candidate espousing those positions. Jackson's earlier statements about the desirability of better relations with the People's Republic also must have been an important element in the initial invitation that came in 1974. While these public positions doubtlessly formed the starting point, they do not account for the kind of relationship that thrived from the initial meeting in 1974.

From the Senator's viewpoint, he was dealing with leaders of a great nation who shared important elements of his own world view, notably the importance of history to an understanding of the present and of the central role of a balance of power in maintaining stability in international relations. On the Chinese side, they clearly appreciated the Senator's concrete efforts to remove specific barriers to better Sino-U.S. relations, but they too must have valued close ties to someone whose world view was in important ways so similar to theirs.

The basis for this understanding was first and foremost the long hours of talks with the Chinese leadership beginning with the Foreign Minister and other senior officials and culminating in meetings with Deng Xiaoping in the Great Hall of the People and in August 1974 with the already very ill Premier Zhou Enlai in his hospital room.

The Senator and Helen were among the last foreign visitors to talk with Zhou Enlai before his death. In fact, the Chinese press announcement of the visit was the first time the Chinese people heard that the Premier was in the hospital. This meeting, during which Zhou spoke of his strong hopes for mutually beneficial Sino-American cooperation, became one of Scoop's most gratifying recollections.

The relationship between the Senator and Deng Xiao-ping turned out to be an unusual and important asset in the development of American relations with China. Two shrewd, pragmatic politicians, each respectful of the other, typically discussed geopolitical and bilateral issues with exceptional frankness and realism.

On each of the four trips to China, Jackson's talks with Chinese leaders averaged fifteen to twenty-four hours spread out over four to five days. In most cases those involved in the initial discussions on the Chinese side briefed those involved in the subsequent talks so that one built on another and unnecessary repetition was avoided.

At the heart of most of these talks, and particularly those with Deng Xiaoping, was a systematic exchange of views on the international security situation around the world. The starting point was relations with the Soviet Union, both those of China and those of the United States, but viewed in a global not a bilateral context. On the 1974 trip, to be sure, the Chinese discoursed eloquently and at length on the shortcomings of the Soviet Union as an ally and on whether or not a million Russian troops on the Sino-Soviet border posed a threat to China. But, most of the discussion was devoted to an analysis of trends in Europe, Asia, and the Middle East and whether those trends were stabilizing influences or whether they were leading to instability that could be exploited by the Soviet Union.

The focus of attention shifted from one trip to another. In 1974, for example, the Chinese were concerned that Pakistan, already reeling from defeat by India and the creation of Bangladesh, would be further dismembered. In 1978, a major Chinese concern was that Egypt and

Sadat would be left out on a limb with inadequate support
from the U.S. In 1979, their principal preoccupation was
with their recently completed incursion into Vietnam. In
1983, the focus was on uncertainties in Sino-Soviet-Ameri-
can relations.

There were significant differences as well as similarities
in the way the Chinese leaders and Senator Jackson approached some of these issues. In the Middle East, the
Chinese started from the proposition that strengthening
those Arabs willing to be independent of the Soviet Union
was crucial. Senator Jackson started from the position that
the security of Israel was the first goal of any Middle East
policy.

There were also differences in view over how the United
States or China could be helpful in bolstering particular
Third World countries. The Senator saw such things as
the American base at Diego Garcia as being essential for
America's position in the Indian Ocean and the Middle
East. The Chinese, while not opposing Diego Garcia, did
not see how it would be of much help to the situation in
Pakistan.

But, both Jackson and the Chinese leaders believed that
despite these differences, the areas of parallel interests of
China and the United States dominated the differences.
Both were strong supporters of NATO. Both saw the importance of a strong Japan with close ties to the United
States. And both felt keenly about the need for a strong,
independent China.

America's interest in a strong, independent China, in
Jackson's view, was not a tactical concern of the moment.
One of the lessons of history, in the Senator's opinion, was
that the United States has long had an interest in a strong,

independent and unified China which contributes to the peace and stability of the Asia-Pacific region. The United States has no reason to threaten China. But the Soviet Union, as the czars before it, cannot welcome the prospect of a strong China at its doorstep. The kind of China which serves Soviet interest is either a unified China under Soviet domination, as the Soviets sought to achieve in the 1950s, or a weak China against which the Soviets can successfully pursue their historic interests in Xinjiang, Mongolia, Manchuria, and Korea. Therefore, Jackson had concluded China will tend to seek closer relations with a nonthreatening sea power from afar rather than with its northern neighbor. The Senator was aware that within the Chinese leadership there could develop factions more favorably disposed toward the Soviet Union than China's present top leaders. But he was basically confident that as long as the United States pursued an intelligent policy toward China the underlying reality would continue to propel the two nations together. As a result, both Washington and Beijing are likely for the years ahead to benefit from consultations about our foreign policies, so that our separate actions in the many areas where our interests overlap would be mutually supportive.

Briefings in Beijing about China's objectives and performance during its incursion into Vietnam in early 1979, for example, illuminated for Jackson both the strengths and limitations of China's then state of military readiness. The dominant Western view then and now was that China's efforts in Vietnam were an expensive failure. The Chinese leaders argued, to the contrary, that they had accomplished at least some of their principal goals. They had demonstrated that they were prepared to act when vital interests were at stake even if that might mean war with the Soviet Union. Furthermore, while the need to root out Vietnamese troops from mountain defenses platoon by platoon had taken longer than anticipated, they did take and destroy a large area before withdrawing. The result, in their view, forced the Vietnamese to expand their armed forces from 600,000 to one million men, a step Vietnam could ill afford. Left unsaid was the fact that all this effort had not caused the Vietnamese to withdraw from Kampuchea.

Senator Jackson, with decades of service on the Senate Armed Services Committee and a knowledge of modern weapons systems, was not converted by these trips and briefings to the advantages of people's war. But he did appreciate better how China was going to cope in the interim period before it had its own modern weapons. And he also saw advantages in China acquiring better defensive weapons, if necessary by purchases from abroad. But he was not an advocate of large-scale arms sales to the Chinese. The Chinese were not likely to want massive purchases, preferring instead to build up their domestic capability. And large-scale purchases would not in any case quickly reverse China's eroding conventional military capacity against the Soviets. More fundamentally, Jackson felt that it was clearly in American interests to assist China to build a strong economy that would better allow China to meet its own defense needs.

Senator Jackson's views on China's strategic role, therefore, were not those of someone interested in using China for short-term tactical maneuvers vis-à-vis the Soviet Union. To the contrary, in his communciations with four Presidents, he continually warned against approaching the

Chinese tactically as a ploy against Moscow. He sensed that such an approach would earn China's scorn and distrust; they would bitterly resent efforts to manipulate them or use them for the end purpose of improving Soviet-American relations. For this reason, he was occasionally critical of Nixon, Ford, Carter, and Reagan for moves which appeared to be tactical in nature.

To be sure, the Senator realized what is abundantly evident—our respective, adversarial relations with Moscow brought us closer together. But, in his view, this could not and should not be the sole basis of a constructive, enduring Sino-American relationship. Senator Jackson believed that the rise of China was an important feature of our era. A century of Western intrusion, civil war, and invasion had come to an end in 1949, and China was now probably embarked on a sustained period of growth which would propel it to the forefront of the world's nations.

The Senator did not express alarm at this development. He believed that, in contrast to Russia, China had historically pursued basically defensive and nonaggressive foreign policies. Moreover, he argued, for China to fail in its developmental objectives would invite the same destabilizing competition among the powers for influence over a weak China as in the late 1800s and early 1900s. Further, since China quite likely would develop with or without American involvement, though at a slower pace, would it not be better for the United States to be involved than not involved? For all these reasons, the Senator attached importance to the forging of extensive economic, scientific and cultural ties between China and the United States. He urged American assistance to China's modernization effort.

BILATERAL RELATIONS

Jackson's advocacy of a strategic relationship with China is easily understood. Less well known is his significant involvement in the promotion of a broad-based bilateral relationship. The events surrounding the Senator's 1978 trip illustrate the point.

Within the United States government in early 1978, the broad issue was whether to push ahead toward the normalization of relations with the People's Republic of China or whether the U.S. should proceed cautiously so as not to derail other foreign policy initiatives. The specific issue was whether the President's National Security Adviser, Zbigniew Brzezinski, would be allowed to visit China.

During his February 1978 talks in Beijing between Jackson and senior Chinese leaders, particularly with Deng Xiaoping, it was clear that the Chinese felt that the momentum toward normalization had been stalled. In their view serious efforts at normalization were not on the U.S. administration's agenda.

In a meeting with President Carter immediately after his return from China, Senator Jackson conveyed his strongly held view that the United States was letting an opportunity of central importance to America's long-term strategic position in the world slip by. The opening paragraphs of his report to the Senate convey the essence of his message.

Despite this reality, and the fact that many of our interests run parallel to those of the Chinese, the United States has not been giving sufficient priority to our own relationship with the People's Republic of China. Our leadership has been preoccupied elsewhere. Only once during the past 2 years has there been any substantial high-level contact between the top leadership of China and of our own executive branch of Government. Our Liaison Office in Peking is too isolated from the Chinese leadership to be an adequate substitute for contact at these highest levels.

On my return from China, I recommended to the President and to the Secretary of State that we should immediately move toward increased and substantial consultation between the most senior officials of our Government and those of China. These consultations at the highest level should take place on a frequent and continuing basis.

Meanwhile, in line with the Shanghai Communique, we should proceed with the process of normalization of relations between our two countries.

Normalization is not the most important aspect of United States-China relations from either an American or a Chinese point of view. For China, the overriding consideration that governs the conduct of their foreign policy is their determination to assure the security of their own country. It was this motivation that led them to seek an improvement of relations with the United States in the first place and it remains today the bedrock upon which the relationship between our two countries rests. For our part, we have a significant stake in the continued existence of a strong, independent China. We share with China a common interest in key strategic issues. We must not let the lack of normalization impede possible progress in areas where our concerns run parallel.

The lack of normalized relations obviously makes working together on common concerns more difficult. I have recommended to the President and to the Secretary of State that a major effort be made to resolve the issues still outstanding that block the full normalization of relations. Normalization must mean the end of diplomatic ties with Taiwan, but should be done in a way that will not jeopardize the peace and stability of the region.[12]

In the early months of 1978 other influential Americans weighed in on one side or the other of this argument, but in May 1978 Brzezinski did go to China with clear instructions to move the normalization process toward completion. And in January 1979, full diplomatic relations between the People's Republic of China and the United States were established.

Normalization, however, did not end the debate over how best to approach China. The immediate issue in the summer of 1979 concerned the trade agreement with China. Although it had been signed in spring 1979, it had not been submitted to the Senate for ratification. The administration was divided over whether to move ahead with China in the absence of the ability to extend most-favored-nation treatment to the Soviet Union. At a press conference at the end of his 1979 China trip and in his October report to the Congress, Jackson reiterated his strong support for immediate ratification.

One key element in our efforts to develop mutually beneficial relations with China will be the trade treaty signed by our two nations that includes a provision for giving China most-favored-nation treatment and opening the way to the granting of credits.

When the Chinese signed the trade agreement on July 7 this year they had been told by top administration officials that the trade agreement, with the Presidential waiver on MFN, would be submitted to the Congress in July. With this promise in mind, the Chinese had affirmed the assurance on freer emigration required by section 402 of the Trade Reform Act of 1974 and modified certain of their negotiating positions on related matters so as not to hold things up and delay the signing. But the administration did not submit the trade agreement to Congress in July.

This is a classic example of how not to treat China.

The administration's conflicting excuses and explanations for the delay and slowdown in the benefits to China of normalization caused serious unhappiness and disappointment in Beijing. Moreover, the delay has advantaged our competitors in Chinese trade, and reduced the momentum in our own trading relationship with China.

One basic difficulty has been the position of key administration officials favoring a policy of "even-handed treatment" of Russia and China. According to this notion, if we give the benefits of MFN and credits to China, we must also give them to the Soviet Union. If China is in conformity with our law and the Soviets not in conformity, then it is argued, efforts must be made to interpret the law to accommodate the country that has chosen not to conform. In the present case, the country that has chosen not to conform is the Soviet Union and the law in question is section 402 of the Trade Reform Act of 1974.

The doctrine of evenhandedness has been at the heart of the administration's delay in submitting the trade agreement to the Congress and at the root of the administration's explanations for the delay.

In fact, China and the Soviet Union are two very different countries at different stages of development, with different interests and ambitions, different associates and allies, and different relations with this country. They should be treated on separate tracks and, in our own national interest, they cannot be treated alike.[13]

Urging that the trade agreement should be promptly submitted to Congress, since China had met the conditions for the waiver of MFN and credits, Jackson went on to say that he was somewhat encouraged that Vice President Mondale had now told the Chinese the trade agreement will be sent to Congress before November 1. Jackson added:

Vice President Mondale's reassurance came just in time to prevent a serious deterioration in Chinese-American relations. Whether the administration—and notably the State Department—has finally shaken itself free of the misguided doctrine of evenhandedness, remains to be seen.[14]

Jackson's intervention built pressure on the administration to move ahead on MFN for China. Support for the trade treaty was only one of the many efforts the Senator made to promote trade between China and the United

States. He was a consistent supporter of making American technology available to China's economic development program particularly in the field of energy.

Sino-American relations worsened in the early years of the Reagan administration, brought on primarily by the President's desire to upgrade relations with Taiwan and by the administration's interest in selling an advanced jet fighter to Taiwan. Jackson did not criticize the administration openly, but he quietly communicated his views to Secretaries of State Haig and Shultz, Secretary of Defense Weinberger, and President Reagan himself. True to his long-term commitment to a bipartisan foreign policy, he refrained from visiting China until he could speak positively about his President's policy and play a constructive role. With the administration's August 1982 agreement with Beijing on U.S. arms sales to Taiwan and with its spring 1983 decision to loosen controls over technology transfer to China—a move Jackson had long advocated—he decided the time had come for another trip. He sought to reassure Deng Xiaoping and other leaders that Reagan's China policy now enjoyed his confidence. He promoted the idea of visits in 1984 by Premier Zhao Ziyang to the United States and by President Reagan to China.

The result of the 1983 trip was to crystallize in his mind the emerging policy issues in the bilateral relationship upon which he hoped to work after his return to Washington, D.C.—a return that never was to be. *First,* he believed that China's energy development was key to its future, and that development was by no means assured. While at Daqing, he sensed the absence of energy conservation technology, and believed enhanced Sino-American cooperation in efficient energy use was an important issue for the

future. *Second,* he was concerned that China was ill-prepared to take maximum advantage of the advanced technologies and equipment available to it. He wanted to think
further about how to enhance Chinese capacity to select
appropriate technologies and to integrate those technologies effectively into their productive processes. *Third,*
as revealed in his Beijing press conference in August 1983,
he believed the August 17, 1982, joint Sino-American communique governing U.S. arms sales to Taiwan called for
the ultimate termination of U.S. weapons sales to the island. He wished to monitor that process and help maintain the American commitment in the communique, on
the assumption China would continue to seek a peaceful
resolution of the issue.

Fourth, he sensed that the growing trade between China
and the United States would require various forms of
financing, and he believed the United States government
would have to be more active in support of American
firms seeking to do business in China. *Finally,* he continued to stress the strategic dimension of Sino-American
relations. He was concerned that more be done to share
our best estimates of the global balance-of-power and to
improve our capacities along these lines. He was sensitive
to the concern of Chinese leaders that U.S.-Soviet arms
control talks might end up with agreements increasing the
already substantial Russian missile threats to China. He
was among the first Americans to pledge resistance to any
agreement that sanctioned taking Soviet SS-20s out of
Europe and adding them to those already adjacent to the
People's Republic. The Senator believed that the dialogue
between leaders of the two countries—in both the public
and private realm—should be expanded and intensified,
so that each side could more effectively take into account

the views of the other, as each pursued its own separate interests. Jackson returned from China in August 1983 with a clear vision of the emerging problems and the direction he hoped the relationship would take.

CONCLUSION

Jackson spent one of his last days in August 1983 in Harbin, the capital of Heilongjiang Province in northeast China. He had gone to Manchuria to acquire a "feel" for this region that bordered on the Soviet Union and to gain a greater understanding of the Sino-Soviet relationship upon which America's security importantly rests. He had read a great deal about the history of the area—of its undetermined future at the turn of the century, of the ensuing struggle among Russia, Japan and China for supremacy in Manchuria, and of how China eventually won the region primarily through the migration of the Han nationality from the poverty and war-struck provinces to the south. The Senator also recalled how, in the mid-20s, over 100,000 Russians had accumulated in Harbin—those who came in the 1890s and 1900s to manage the Russian-built Chinese Railway, then the White Russians fleeing the revolution, and finally the Red Russians in the mid-20s protecting Soviet interests.

Henry Jackson held his traveling companions spellbound as he recounted this history at breakfast. Then he asked his Chinese hosts to take him on a tour of the city, so he could better envision and understand past events. He stumbled upon an old and recently refurbished Protestant church and had a moving meeting with the pastor. He wandered in a teeming market place. He looked at a refurbished monument to Soviet soldiers who "liberated" Harbin from Japanese control in 1945. At the end of the long day, he boarded the overnight pullman express to visit the pivotal coastal city of Dalian.

In the last decade of his career, China had become a central part of Senator Jackson's world view. No real understanding of the possibilities for peace and stability were possible unless they included China, not simply as a counter to the Soviet Union, but as a great nation in its own right. And, no real understanding of China was possible unless one took the trouble to study its history and culture as well as its current policies.

Thus, it was not an accident that the Senator was such a strong supporter of the School of International Studies at the University of Washington with its three-quarter century of research and teaching the history, politics, economics, and languages of China, the Soviet Union and other major areas. This school now bears his name—The Henry M. Jackson School of International Studies—just the kind of active, relevant memorial the Senator would have welcomed and relished.

The Central America Commission

RYAN MALARKEY

Ryan Malarkey became a professional staff member of the Senate Committee on Foreign Relations in April 1985.

He first worked with Senator Jackson in Washington State as King County Coordinator for the Jackson 1982 campaign for the Senate. He joined the Senator's staff in Washington, D.C. in February 1983 as legislative assistant with special responsibility for international trade problems, and Central American issues including the gestation of what became the bipartisan Central America Commission. Following his service with the Senator he was on the staff of the Bureau of Human Rights in the Department of State. BA 1978 University of Oregon.

The Mexican Deputy Foreign Minister and Ambassador had been kept waiting in the reception area of Senator Jackson's office for twenty minutes. Their stated purpose was to learn more about Senator Jackson's call for a national bipartisan commission on Central America. In fact, their curiosity centered on the Senator's constant reference to Mexico as the true target of communist aggression in the region. As I delivered yet another apology for the Senator's delay, word arrived that Scoop could not get far from the Senate floor and would meet the visitors in the Lyndon Baines Johnson Room in the Capitol.

Used by the Democrats for their regular Tuesday policy luncheons, the room has little of the grandeur of many Senate chambers. An impressive chandelier hangs from the ceiling, but there is also the stale smell of tobacco from cigar burns in the rug. On the day the Mexicans visited, piled up chairs and other leftovers from an earlier lunch littered the place. None of this fazed Senator Jackson. The room was convenient and offered more privacy than the crowded Senate reception chamber. The Senate was in the early legislative frenzy of 1983, and anyone would understand.

As the Mexican diplomats were escorted over to the Capitol from the Hart Office Building, they received a lesson in the right of citizens to petition their government. In summer, the grounds crawl with tourists, many practicing first-hand lobbying on whatever member of Congress

173

they recognize. Visibly surprised by the hordes of every-
day Americans, the Mexican officials somehow survived
the battle for seats on the subway and the crush in the
elevator to the second floor of the Capitol. But I doubt
they soon got over their surprise at the unconventional,
undiplomatic atmosphere of the Johnson Room.

In general, Senator Jackson avoided ambassadorial
meetings. They often entailed special pleading by a foreign government on issues which were handled more ap-
propriately through executive branch channels. But Mexico was pivotal in Senator Jackson's analysis of Central
America. Long-term stability in the region hinged on
Mexico maintaining its own stability by living up to its self-
image as a modern, industrialized nation playing a diplomatic role commensurate with its status.

In more subtle terms, this is precisely the message Senator Jackson conveyed to the Mexicans. His call for a
commission, he assured them, intended no abrupt, unilateral U.S. initiatives for Central America. He had proposed that the commission consult closely with the nations
of the region, especially Mexico. Given Mexican skit-
tishness when the United States ignores Mexico, or worse
still, when we pay attention to it, the meeting went well.

After the diplomats departed, I mentioned to the Senator
our visitors' reaction to seeing the Capitol building teeming
with American tourists. Senator Jackson responded, "Well,
you know, Ryan, Spanish tradition has given a lot of things to
the world, but democracy isn't one of them."

THE DOMESTIC CONTEXT OF THE COMMISSION

In the spring of 1983, when Senator Jackson publicly
broached the idea of a bipartisan, citizen-based commis-

sion on Central America, the Reagan administration was still coping with Secretary of State Haig's well-intentioned but insufficient and oversimplified depiction of the Central America conflict as a contest between East and West. The administration's policy-making apparatus was in disarray with one special envoy to Central America after another being appointed. Executive branch agencies constantly second-guessed one another.

The administration also seemed bent on misreading the public. For most Americans, the most salient feature of the region was not the communist threat, but Central America's unremitting poverty, its corrupt elites, and its gross social inequities. Yet in trying to get security assistance through Congress, the administration put its main emphasis on military aid requirements in the context of the communist threat. It expended enormous amounts of political capital in the process, and by failing to bring up front and center the serious social and economic injustices of the area, it risked losing both needed economic and security assistance for the region.

The incoherence in Congress was even worse. In a debate framed principally by liberal Democrats, discourse about Central America and the administration's proposals had been reduced to sterile arguments over whether one favored "military" versus "political" solutions to Central American conflicts. Congressional attention focused on the conditions of assistance and the next quarterly human rights certification, rarely on our overall strategic interests, and the long-term policy required to protect them.

Important voices in Congress were still giving the Sandinista regime the benefit of the doubt, finding the principal cause of Sandinista repression (including repression of the Church and labor unions) in U.S. support of the "contras" rather than in the intrinsic Leninist nature of the regime. Ignoring Nicaragua's massive arms build-up from East Bloc assistance, liberal Democrats regularly accused the Reagan administration of "militarizing" the region, and consumed hours of debate over the politico-military significance of 55 U.S. military advisers in El Salvador versus some lesser number. Hours were also spent conducting a taxonomy of the Salvadoran armed insurgency (the FMLN), and its political arm, the FDR, trying to determine which faction was "really" communist and which wasn't. Many members of Congress wanted to rush to judgment on whether the Salvadoran government was worth defending or not. If not, as the question implied, their goal was to have the United States force the creation of a coalition government in El Salvador hoping that the perceived democratic elements of the FMLN/FDR would somehow prevail.

All of this suggested a major foreign policy disaster in the making, but it also faced Senator Jackson with a pressing political problem. Confronting the redoubtable rhetorical skills of President Reagan, Senator Jackson's fellow Democrats constantly came to him for advice and guidance. Too few of them shared his own principal political concern: Democrats were positioning themselves so far out on a leftward limb that in the process of losing sight of sound policy, they were also losing sight of sound politics.

Worse still, in this environment, the disputes grew ever more partisan and personal. Many members, especially House Democrats, wanted to make litmus tests of party loyalty out of the unceasing votes on security assistance. For someone with Senator Jackson's staunch belief in bipartisanship in vital national security matters, it signaled that hopes for restructuring a dominant, two-party political center on important foreign policy issues in the post-Vietnam era were rapidly evaporating.

In large measure, the idea of the commission was born from the pragmatic difficulties confronting Senator Jackson daily. The debate in Congress had grown so rancorous, and the administration had so over-reached with its bellicose rhetoric, that the desperately needed legislation providing economic and security assistance was imperiled. And unless something was done that would allow the aid packages to move forward, there was little chance that the United States could ever find its way to consensus on an effective, sustainable policy.

THE GEOPOLITICAL CONTEXT

Alarming as the breakdown of consensus on Central America was in itself, it was made worse by the region's overwhelming strategic importance to the United States. Senator Jackson had participated in many critical debates and votes on Central American issues, including support for ratification of the Panama Canal treaties, but over the years, like others, he had not given the area his special and concentrated attention. The Atlantic Community, the Middle East, U.S.-Soviet relations, arms control, and China consumed most of his foreign policy time. But, with others, he paid more attention to the region as the Sandinistas displayed their true colors and the communist rebels in El Salvador grew more effective as the regime grew more repressive. His real point of entry to the Central American debate, however, was not the political disintegration of the Central American isthmus itself, but the impending economic collapse of Mexico.

The 1982 world recession hung over the entire Central American debate in the spring of 1983. The economies of the region were virtually prostrate, and economic decline, much less communist insurgency, threatened their governments. Hopeful in the belief that Mexico's sole ruling party for over 50 years, the Institutional Revolutionary Party, or PRI, would long serve as the basis for stability in Mexico, Senator Jackson had his confidence shaken by the Mexican debt crisis in August 1982.

As ranking member of the Senate Energy Committee, Senator Jackson played an important role in the international emergency rescue package for Mexico in August 1982. The package, which helped prevent international financial panic, included prepayment to Mexico for oil to fill the Strategic Petroleum Reserve. Close to the negotiations over a long, tense weekend, Senator Jackson appreciated how close the Mexican crisis came to precipitating a collapse of the entire international financial system. Already consulting almost daily with well-known Wall Street analysts, Senator Jackson paid even closer attention to the interconnections between the debt crisis, political stability in the developing world, and their consequences for U.S. foreign policy and strategic thinking.

Mexico loomed larger and larger on his horizon, and it led him to urge his Senate colleagues to pay more attention to the stability of our southern neighbor. In his major floor statement on May 12, 1983 calling for the Central America Commission, Mexico consumed nearly half of the speech. He warned his colleagues at the time that "the institution responsible for Mexican stability since the revolution—the PRI, the Institutional Revolutionary Party—has never confronted such a challenging set of circumstances as it does today or is likely to in the near future."[1]

In speech after speech, he never tired of telling his audiences that if you counted Mexico as part of Central America, it constituted 76 percent of the land mass and 79 percent of the population.

But his major message about Mexico was strategic. On a Sunday morning news show, he averred that the true target of those fomenting subversion in Central America was Mexico. The remark received wide media coverage, including in Europe. He based his charge on logic and on intelligence indicating the degree to which Mexico's regime had been penetrated by long-term Soviet and Cuban agents. Later, he told several on his staff, "You talk about El Salvador, and Americans don't care; you talk about Mexico and they pay attention! If you were Stalin and looking at a map, which country in the Western hemisphere would you have targeted for subversion? Trotsky wasn't the only thing he was hunting for there."

He continued to spell out the threat in private talks with his colleagues. In his May 12 speech on the Senate floor, he warned:

A sequence of crises leading to Castro-type regimes throughout Central America, including Mexico, would have disastrous strategic ramifications which we all recognize. None of us relishes the prospect of living in a garrison state, unable to meet our commitments to our NATO allies and others, nor do we like to contemplate the threat such a course of events poses to the fundamental nature of American society and her institutions.[2]

THE COMMISSION AS EXPEDIENT

It is ironic that in order to contain the centrifugal effects of the domestic debate on Central America, Senator Jackson proposed a commission, for he lacked enthusiasm for them in principle. Responsibility for the conduct of foreign relations, he believed, was centered in the President and his first adviser, the Secretary of State—accountable under the Constitution to the Congress. In his landmark Subcommittee study of national security policy-making, he had argued against the notion that the poor performance of one organization can be cured by creating another. He evidenced a basic skepticism toward novel additions to the policy process such as super-NSC level planning staffs, strategy boards, blue-ribbon councils of wise men and new committees. Indeed, in his 1961 summary statement of the study, he said, "Committee killing, not creating more committees, remains the important job."[3]

Senator Jackson's decision to propose a commission for Central America indicated how seriously he viewed the inability of the center within our political culture to hold together on this vital national security issue. He believed an ad hoc expedient was needed to bolster a consensus— at least temporarily. It is no accident that his choice as his first audience before which to present the idea of a commission was the American labor movement.

In addressing a labor law conference on April 24, 1983, in honor of Eddie Carlough, long-time President of the Sheet Metal Workers Union, the Senator said:

> Security assistance [to Central America] ought not to be the main focus of national debate, and it ought not to be the foreign policy instrument we emphasize to the rest of the world.
> Our security aid . . . should be given and discussed in one way: it is a shield behind which endangered nations can protect themselves from external threats while they go about the business of building democratic institutions, holding free and fair elections, and working to rectify historical patterns of social injustice. Security assistance should be an adjunct to our Central American

policy, not its foundation. We better face it: the shield will crumble unless we address the serious social and economic injustices in the region.[4]

Labor was one of the last institutions that represented the old consensus on U.S. foreign policy. It easily understood Senator Jackson's insistence that Central America's problems be seen whole. The multiple threats to democracy in Central America—poverty and social inequities exploited by communist insurgents—needed to be tackled simultaneously, not on an ad hoc, country-by-country basis. Firmly anti-communist, but holding deep concern for Central America's cruel history of social injustice, the American labor movement provided the model for what he believed the administration policy approach should be.

The Reagan administration's seeming inability to work with American labor on foreign policy issues frustrated him enormously. He was simply dismayed that American labor's links to Europe's social democratic parties weren't being used effectively in the battle for the hearts and minds of Europe's successor generation. My first direct assignment from the Senator came after he returned from an intelligence briefing on Vietnam's use of chemical agents in Laos and Cambodia, dumbfounded that the administration had no sensible plan for using the information in an effective way in Europe, particularly with the democratic left. He described how he had to lecture the administration witnesses on the crucial role of the American labor movement in saving postwar European social democratic parties from communist takeover. He requested that I get full transcripts of the historic debates between Britain's great labor leader and Foreign Minister, Ernest Bevin, and the Soviet Commissar for Foreign Affairs, Molotov, at the early United Nations meetings in Flushing Meadows, New York. He then asked the staff around him, "Don't they understand that history?"

American labor, he believed, was uniquely suited to serve as the nucleus around which other segments of American society could gather to reach consensus on Central American policy. As he told the labor law conference honoring Eddie Carlough:

> In El Salvador, the American labor movement has been one of the few beacons of light in what seemed an interminable darkness. . . .
>
> Into this almost intractable situation, where all the policy options seem impalatable, the AFL-CIO, through its American Institute for Free Labor Development, went forward and labored hard to bring about reform. . . .
>
> The general approach to addressing El Salvador's long-term problems has been charted by the AFL-CIO.[5]

Senator Jackson spent considerable effort spelling out how he believed the commission should be composed and how it should be launched. In several speeches he stressed that it should be a broad-based citizen commission of business, labor, academic, and Hispanic leaders from different regions of the country joined by the participation of leading members of Congress from both parties. As a demonstration not only of its bipartisan nature, but the breadth of the political spectrum he wished represented, he asked Senator Charles McC. Mathias to join him as principal cosponsor of a Senate resolution calling for the commission. Senator Mathias, a liberal Republican, differed with Senator Jackson on many foreign policy matters—notably in the arms control area—but he was regarded by his colleagues as one of the chamber's most intelligent members, and well informed in general on foreign policy. Senator

Jackson respected, in particular, Senator Mathias' abiding commitment to maintaining cohesion in the Atlantic Community.

The Jackson/Mathias Senate resolution was introduced in the House by two members from opposite ends of the political spectrum, Democrat Mike Barnes of Maryland and Republican Jack Kemp of New York. Meanwhile, Senator Jackson had been in steady touch with the White House urging favorable action on the commission—the sooner the better. His strategy worked. Before either resolution had time to be considered in the legislative process, President Reagan took up the idea and decided to appoint a commission with Henry Kissinger as its chairman and named the four legislative sponsors of the resolutions as senior counsellors.

Senator Jackson died just as the commission had begun its work. It is impossible to say whether he would have agreed with all of its recommendations, or that, if he had lived, the commission's work would have been paid greater attention. But the commission dedicated its final report to him and said in tribute, "In his life and work Senator Jackson was devoted to the twin goals of national security and human betterment. These are also the goals that have guided this report, and we hope, in his spirit that it will contribute to their advancement."[6]

Senator Jackson had fully realized the complexity and intractability of the problems in Central America—with its seven independent countries, constrained by their own history and their special circumstances and temptations. But he was a firm believer that a great democratic power, leader of the Western alliance, must accept its responsibilities, neither flee from them nor fritter them away. He was convinced that a careful, sure-footed use of American influence could help safeguard freedom in this hemisphere and foster a more surely democratic and humane future for the peoples of the region.

The commission was a contrivance for Senator Jackson to help lift the Central America debate above its current level of bitterness and stalemate in the hopes that enough consensus could be developed to allow the President and the Congress to forge an effective and sustainable assistance policy. He knew only too well that the usefulness of any commission depended not only on the quality of its findings but on whether the President and Congress would follow through and build the necessary political support for them.

In a penetrating essay written after Senator Jackson's death, Charles Krauthammer described the significance of the commission as a symptom of its time:

> No doubt, *ad hoc* centrism is better than none. But it is at best a temporary and incomplete solution to a structural flaw in American politics. In the meantime, until it is corrected, until the liberal internationalist tradition can rebuild itself into a political force, we can look forward to more oscillatory democracy and, to dampen its abrupt left-right swings, more commissions.[7]

Postscript

DOROTHY FOSDICK

He missed the ultimate prize of our politics, perhaps because he lacked the crackling temperament that marks persons who burn on the surface with a hard, gemlike flame. If his political metabolism seemed uncommonly calm, that is because he had the patience of a mature politician—a gift for planning, thirst for detail, and a sense of ripeness in issues. He had a flame, but he had depth in which he kept it. —*George Will's address at the Washington, D.C. Memorial Service for Senator Jackson, September 6, 1983.*[1]

Henry Jackson twice sought the White House, campaigning vigorously for the Democratic nomination. The question arises: Why didn't this man of Presidential caliber succeed in this venture? George Will suggests it was perhaps due to some lack of public flame or charisma. Many others think that the Senator's strong views on national defense and foreign policy played a principal role—in the political climate that existed in 1972 and 1976—in denying him the chance to be his party's nominee. In either case, Scoop was not one to desert his convictions to meet the vagaries of current opinion. On matters related to the survival of the nation and its human values, like Edmund Burke, he believed he owed the people his best judgment.

The story of Jackson's tries for the White House is not included in this book. However, these essays do provide important background for a full treatment of the Senator's view of the office of the Presidency, and some insight into his aspiration to occupy that office.

187

Scoop emerged on the national scene during an era of unprecedented challenge to America's safety and values. Over a long and dangerous period he rallied Americans to accept their world responsibilities—and not run from them. The Atlantic Alliance he staunchly championed has securely protected the West from aggression for over four decades. Approaches he staked out on other national security issues not only remain relevant but in some cases they are becoming even more important.

Moreover, Scoop left a lively legacy. A notable number of his associates and his staff have gone on to distinguished careers in government, academia, law and the media.

Today, members of Congress and others invoke the Jackson name on behalf of a variety of causes. Prominent politicians, leaders in other professions, and legions of Americans proudly declare that they are "in the Jackson tradition," or that they are "Jackson Democrats" or "Jackson Republicans." Those who so refer to themselves are confident that they know what basic values and public policy approaches Jackson represents and are proud in personally identifying with them. The terms "Jackson tradition," "Jackson Democrat," "Jackson Republican" have thus entered the language of the West, and, I suspect, the language of other nations, including China and the Soviet Union.

This understanding among so many—including serious students of domestic and international policy—of what "Henry M. Jackson" stands for is reassuring. People at home and abroad—including some of the Senator's most severe past critics—see him looming larger and larger in the perspective of history. And history, assisted by time, is softening the edges of the once harsh caricatures and is moving them into a humorous context.

During the final decade of his life, the Senator became increasingly convinced that the U.S.-Sino-Soviet relationship and its management was the key to the future of world stability and personal freedom. He saw little chance that the United States could successfully manage U.S. interests in this critical relationship unless our future leaders had an in-depth understanding of the history of both nations and of Sino-Russian relations, as well as the past experience of the adjacent nations in Asia and the Middle East. Jackson was deeply interested in and committed to encouraging the development of such understanding through higher education and advanced scholarship.

This partly explains Scoop's personal commitment to the School of International Studies at his alma mater, the University of Washington. Colleagues and friends were constantly regaled with the story of the School's 75-year record in the study of the history, politics, economics and languages of the world's major regions—especially Asia, the Soviet bloc and the Middle East. A few days before Scoop died he was laying plans for a renewed personal effort to markedly increase the School's academic endowment and to enhance its national role. No posthumous recognition would have contented him more than the renaming of this distinguished school in his honor—The Henry M. Jackson School of International Studies. And it is fitting that the Henry M. Jackson Foundation, established in October 1983 by Helen Jackson and friends and colleagues of the Senator to commemorate his public service, is following up on his long-range educational concerns—giving priority to substantial support for the

Jackson School, and encouraging its development as an indispensable national asset.

Winston Churchill once said that he had only one question about the future: Will America stay the course? This became a favorite Jackson quotation and a challenge he repeatedly put to Presidents, his colleagues in the Congress and the American people: "Do we have the will to stay the course? That is the fundamental question."

The Senator had a great faith in America. But he was profoundly aware that the cause of freedom is long term, defying being dealt with once and for all, demanding unremitting care and vigilance, with victories won only by perseverance. In his words: "If you believe in freedom, then proclaim it, live it, and protect it, for humanity's future depends upon it."

Notes

INTRODUCTION

1. George F. Will, "The Finest Public Servant I Have Known" (September 6, 1983). In *The Morning After; American Successes and Excesses 1981–1986* (New York: The Free Press, 1986), p. 410.

2. Ted Stevens, informal remarks at a reception for members of the Henry M. Jackson Foundation Congressional Advisory Council, Office of the Majority Whip of the House of Representatives, U.S. Capitol, 15 May 1984.

3. Charles Krauthammer, "Whatever Became of the American Center?" In *Cutting Edges; Making Sense of the 80's* (New York: Random House, 1985), p. 95.

4. Howard H. Baker, Jr., tribute on the floor of the Senate. In *Henry M. Jackson; Late a Senator from Washington* (Washington, D.C.: Government Printing Office, 1983), p. 24.

5. Henry M. Jackson, "A Time to Stress Excellence," commencement address, Carroll College, Helena, Montana, 6 May 1973. Jackson Papers, University of Washington Libraries, Seattle.

6. Anna Marie Jackson, remarks at the Family Memorial Service for Senator Henry M. Jackson, The First Presbyterian Church, Everett, Washington. In *Henry M. Jackson; Late a Senator from Washington* (Washington, D.C.: Government Printing Office, 1983), p. 36.

7. Cited, for example: Henry M. Jackson, "Does America Have a Peace Strategy?" remarks at the Plymouth Congregational Church, Seattle, Washington, 4 June 1982. Jackson Papers, University of Washington Libraries, Seattle.

THE EARLY YEARS

1. U.S., Congress, House, Concurrent Resolution 219, 81st Cong., 2d sess., 6 June 1950, *Congressional Record* 96:8206.

U.S., Congress, House, Concurrent Resolution 162, 82d Cong., 1st sess., 18 September 1951, *Congressional Record* 97:11572.

U.S., Congress, Senate, Concurrent Resolution 27, 83d Cong., 1st sess., 1 May 1953, *Congressional Record* 99:4279.

2. Henry M. Jackson, "Declassified Recommendations on the IBM submitted to President Dwight D. Eisenhower by Senator Clinton Anderson and Senator Henry M. Jackson with covering letter of 30 June 1955 and the President's reply of 7 July 1955," press release, 14 October 1957. Jackson Papers, University of Washington Libraries, Seattle.

3. Senator Jackson initially discussed his proposal for a joint U.S.-USSR Information Communications Risk Reduction Center with mem-

bers of the press in April 1982. See: Edwin M. Yoder, Jr., "The Jackson Alternative," *Washington Post,* 19 April 1982, sec. A, p. 11. Also: Face the Nation, CBS Network Interview, Washington, D.C., 25 April 1982.

4. Edmund Burke, "The Duty of a Representative." In *Edmund Burke on Revolution,* Robert A. Smith, ed. (New York: Harper and Row, 1968) as cited in: U.S., Congress, Senate, Committee on Government Operations, Subcommittee on National Security and International Operations, *Councils and Committees; A Selection of Readings.* Committee Print, 92d Cong., 2d sess., 1972, p. 23.

THE JACKSON SUBCOMMITTEE ON NATIONAL SECURITY

1. Henry M. Jackson, "How Shall We Forge a Strategy for Survival?" address at the National War College, Washington, D.C., 16 April 1959. Jackson Papers, University of Washington Libraries, Seattle.

2. U.S., Congress, Senate, statement by Senator Jackson on the floor of the Senate 14 July 1959 upon introduction of Senate Resolution 115. Cited in: Committee on Government Operations, Subcommittee on National Policy Machinery, *Organizing for National Security, Vol. 1, Hearings,* 86th Cong., 2d sess., p. 5.

3. U.S., Congress, Senate, Committee on Government Operations, Subcommittee on National Policy Machinery, *Organizing for National Security, Vol. 1, Hearings.* 86th Cong,. 2d sess., 24 February 1960, pp. 12–45.

4. Cabell Phillips, "'Subtle Spectacular' on Capitol Hill," *New York Times Magazine,* 29 May 1960, p. 18.

5. U.S., Congress, Senate, Committee on Government Operations, Subcommittee on National Policy Machinery, *Organizing for National Security, Vol. 3, Staff Reports and Recommendations,* 87th Cong., 1st sess., 1961, p. 37.

6. Henry M. Jackson, "Introduction." In *The National Security Council; Jackson Subcommittee Papers on Policy-Making at the Presidential Level,* Henry M. Jackson, ed. (New York: Frederick A. Praeger, Inc., 1965), p. xiii.

7. *Organizing for National Security, Vol. 3, Staff Reports and Recommendations,* 1961, p. 4.

8. Henry M. Jackson, "Introduction." In *The Secretary of State and the Ambassador; Jackson Subcommittee Papers on the Conduct of American Foreign Policy,* Henry M. Jackson, ed. (New York: Frederick A. Praeger, Inc., 1964), p. vii.

9. Ibid., p. 14.

10. Ibid., p. 65.

11. *Organizing for National Security, Vol. 1, Hearings.* 86th Cong., 2d sess., 10 June 1960, pp. 696–726.

12. U.S., Congress, Senate, Committee on Government Operations, Subcommittee on National Security and International Operations,

Specialists and Generalists: A Selection of Readings. Committee Print, 90th Cong., 2d sess., 1968.

13. Henry M. Jackson, ed., *The Atlantic Alliance; Jackson Subcommittee Hearings and Findings* (New York: Frederick A. Praeger, Inc., 1967).

14. Ibid., p. 200.

15. Ibid., p. xii.

16. U.S., Congress, Senate, Committee on Government Operations, *International Negotiation, Hearings before the Subcommittee on National Security and International Operations,* part 2, 91st Cong., 2d sess., 16 April 1970, p. 29.

17. U.S., Congress, Senate, Committee on Government Operations, Subcommittee on National Security and International Operations, *International Negotiation; Exchanges of Scholars with the Soviet Union: Advantages and Dilemmas.* Committee Print, 91st Cong., 1st sess., 1969.

18. U.S., Congress, Senate, Committee on Government Operations, Subcommittee on National Security and International Operations, *Negotiation and Statecraft; A Selection of Readings.* 91st Cong., 2d sess. 1970, pp. 52–3.

JACKSON: FOREIGN AFFAIRS GENERALIST

1. Henry M. Jackson, "Seven Assumptions that Beset Us," *New York Times Magazine,* 4 August 1963, p. 9. Reprinted: Henry M. Jackson, *Fact, Fiction and National Security* (New York: McFadden-Bartell Corporation, 1964), p. 103.

2. U.S., Congress, Senate, comments by Senator Jackson during debate on "The Military Selective Service Act," 92d Cong., 1st sess., 13 May 1971, *Congressional Record* 117:14893.

3. U.S., Congress, Senate, "The Race for the Ballistic Missile," statement by Senator Jackson on the floor of the Senate, 84th Cong., 2d sess., 1 February 1956, *Congressional Record* 102:1763–65.

4. Henry M. Jackson, "The Balance of Power and the Future of Freedom," address to the Coalition for a Democratic Majority Friends of Freedom Awards Dinner honoring Andrei Sakharov, Washington, D.C., 24 April 1980. See: U.S., Congress, Senate, 96th Cong., 2d sess., 6 May 1980, *Congressional Record* 126:10094–95.

5. U.S., Congress, Senate, comments by Senator Jackson during debate on "U.S. Forces in Europe," 89th Cong., 2d sess., 1 September 1966, *Congressional Record* 112:21577.

6. Henry M. Jackson, speech to the Seattle Rotary Club, Seattle, Washington, 5 November 1969. Jackson Papers, University of Washington Libraries, Seattle.

7. Interview with editors and reporters of the *Washington Post,* Washington, D.C., 21 November 1971. Jackson Papers, University of Washington Libraries, Seattle.

8. Henry M. Jackson, remarks at the Naval Air Station, Seattle, Washington, 6 April 1968. Jackson Papers, University of Washington Libraries, Seattle.

9. Letter to President Richard M. Nixon initiated by Senator Henry M. Jackson and Senator Hugh Scott, and cosigned by 28 other Senators, 1 September 1970. Jackson Papers, University of Washington Libraries, Seattle.

10. Interview with editors and reporters of the *Washington Post*, Washington, D.C., 21 November 1971. Jackson Papers, University of Washington Libraries, Seattle.

11. Henry M. Jackson, "Introduction." In *The National Security Council; Jackson Subcommittee Papers on Policy-Making at the Presidential Level*, Henry M. Jackson, ed. (New York: Frederick A. Praeger, Inc., 1965), p. xii.

12. Peter H. Jackson, remarks at the Launching of the Trident Submarine, HENRY M. JACKSON SSBN 70, 15 October 1983, Groton, Connecticut.

THE SENATOR AND AMERICAN ARMS CONTROL POLICY

1. Senator Jackson voted for every arms control agreement that was reported to the Senate for a final vote during his service there.

—He voted for the earliest of the post-World War II arms limitation agreements, the Antarctic Treaty which demilitarized the Antarctic Continent. 86th Cong., 2d sess., 10 August 1960, *Congressional Record* 106:16114.

—He voted for legislation in President Kennedy's first year establishing the U.S. Arms Control and Disarmament Agency. 87th Cong., 1st sess., 8 September 1961, *Congressional Record* 107:18755.

—He voted for President Kennedy's Limited Nuclear Test-Ban Treaty which banned nuclear weapons tests in the atmosphere, outer space and under water. 88th Cong., 1st sess., 24 September 1963, *Congressional Record* 109:17832.

—He voted for President Johnson's Treaty on Outer Space which limits use of the moon and other celestial bodies exclusively to peaceful purposes. 90th Cong., 1st sess., 25 April 1967, *Congressional Record* 113:10687.

—In President Nixon's first year, he voted for the Nuclear Non-Proliferation Treaty to ban spread of nuclear weapons. 91st Cong., 1st sess., 13 March 1969, *Congressional Record* 115:6380.

—Also during President Nixon's term, he voted for a resolution of ratification of Protocol II to the Treaty of Tlatelolco, a treaty to prohibit the production, testing or possession of nuclear weapons in Latin America. 92d Cong., 1st sess., 19 April 1971, *Congressional Record* 117:10745.

—He supported and announced in favor of President Nixon's Seabed Arms Control Treaty which bans the deployment of nuclear weapons or other weapons of mass destruction on the ocean floor. 92d Cong., 2d sess., 15 February 1972, *Congressional Record* 118:3958.

—He voted for President Nixon's Treaty on the Limitation of Anti-Ballistic Missile Systems. 92d Cong., 2d sess., 3 August 1972, *Congressional Record* 118:26770.

—Again, he voted for President Nixon's SALT I agreement on limiting offensive nuclear weapons. 92d Cong., 2d sess. 14 September 1972, *Congressional Record* 118:30665–66.

—In the Ford administration, he voted for the Geneva Protocol prohibiting the first use of chemical/gas weapons. 93d Cong., 2d sess., 16 December 1974, *Congressional Record* 120:40067–68.

—He also voted during the Ford administration for the Biological Weapons Convention of 1972 which prohibits the development, manufacture and acquisition of biological agents or toxins and orders the destruction of existing stocks. 93d Cong., 2d sess., 16 December 1974, *Congressional Record* 120:40068.

—In President Ford's second year, he voted for the Protocol to the Treaty on the limitation of Anti-Ballistic Missile Systems which further limits ABM deployment. 94th Cong., 1st sess., 10 November 1975, *Congressional Record* 121:35721–22.

—He voted for President Carter's Convention on the Prohibition of Military or any Other Hostile Use of Environmental Modification Techniques. 96th Cong., 1st sess., 28 November 1979, *Congressional Record* 125:33818.

2. William Beecher, "Senators Seek to Bolster U.S. Arms-Pact Position," *New York Times,* 3 August 1972, p. 1.

3. Henry M. Jackson, "Detente and SALT," address at the Overseas Press Club, New York, New York, 22 April 1974. See: U.S., Congress, Senate, 93d Cong., 2d sess., 23 April 1974, *Congressional Record* 120:11301–2.

4. U.S., Congress, Senate, Committee on Armed Services, *Military Implications of the Proposed SALT II Treaty relating to the National Defense.* S. Rept. 96–1054, 96th Cong., 2d sess., 1980.

HUMAN RIGHTS AND THE JACKSON AMENDMENT

1. U.S., Congress, Senate, Committee on Government Operations, Permanent Subcommittee on Investigations, *International Human Rights; Selected Statements and Initiatives.* Committee Print, 95th Cong., 1st sess., 1977, p. III.

2. *Freedom of emigration in East-West Trade, U.S. Code,* vol. 19, sec. 2432 (1975).

3. U.S., Congress, Senate, Open Letter to the United States Congress from Andrei Sakharov, 93d Cong., 2d sess., 13 December 1974, *Congressional Record* 120:39786.

4. U.S., Congress, Senate, Exchange of Letters Between Secretary Kissinger and Senator Jackson, 93d Cong., 2d sess., 13 December 1974, *Congressional Record* 120:39785–86.

5. U.S., Congress, Senate, Committee on Finance, *Emigration Amendment to the Trade Reform Act of 1974, Hearing before the full Committee.* 93d Cong., 2d sess., 3 December 1974, pp. 51–112.

6. David Remnick, "Shcharansky Meets Reagan; 'Quiet Diplomacy' Unchanged," *Washington Post,* 14 May 1986, sec. A., p. 1.

7. Mike Harvey, "Scoop." In *Henry M. Jackson; Late a Senator from Washington* (Washington, D.C.: Government Printing Office, 1983), p. 187.

8. Henry M. Jackson, "The Balance of Power and the Future of Freedom," address to the Coalition for a Democratic Majority Friends of Freedom dinner honoring Andrei Sakharov, Washington, D.C., 24 April 1980. See: U.S., Congress, Senate, 96th Cong., 2d sess., 6 May 1980, *Congressional Record* 126:10094–95.

9. U.S., President, *Weekly Compilation of Presidential Documents,* Remarks on Awarding the [Presidential] Medal [of Freedom] to the late Senator Henry M. Jackson, (Washington, D.C.: Office of the *Federal Register,* National Archives and Records Service, 2 July 1984), Ronald R. Reagan, 1984, 20:941.

SENATOR JACKSON
AND THE U.S. RELATIONSHIP WITH ISRAEL

1. Henry M. Jackson, remarks at the Coalition for a Democratic Majority Human Rights Dinner, New York, New York, 30 September 1978. Jackson Papers, University of Washington Libraries, Seattle.

THE CHINA POLICY OF HENRY JACKSON

1. The summary of Senator Jackson's posture on China in the 1950s and 1960s is based on recollections which he shared with the authors, and on their conversations with those who worked with the Senator at the time. Jackson's remarks on China contained in the *Congressional Record* were also surveyed.

2. U.S., Congress, Senate, Committee on Government Operations, Subcommittee on National Policy Machinery, *National Policy Machinery in Communist China.* S. Rept. 86–1096, 86th Cong., 2d sess., 1960.

3. U.S., Congress, Senate, statement by Senator Jackson during debate on "U.S. Policy Toward China," 89th Cong., 2d sess., 3 May 1966, *Congressional Record* 112:9605.

4. Henry M. Jackson, "The End of the Beginning," commencement address at Whitman College, Walla Walla, Washington, 5 June 1966. Jackson Papers, University of Washington Libraries, Seattle.

5. U.S., Congress, Senate, "U.S. Obligations in Asia," statement by Senator Jackson on the floor of the Senate, 89th Cong., 2d sess., 28 July 1966, *Congressional Record* 112:17433–34.

6. Henry M. Jackson, "New Directions in the Pacific Area," address to the Seattle Rotary Club, Seattle, Washington, 5 November 1969. See: U.S., Congress, Senate, 91st Cong., 1st sess., 1 December 1969, *Congressional Record* 115:36173–74.

7. U.S., Congress, Senate, Committee on Government Operations, Subcommittee on National Security and International Operations, *Peking's Approach to Negotiations; Selected Writings.* Committee Print, 91st Cong., 1st sess., 1969. Note: The pamphlet was signed for publication on March 10, 1969 and instructions to prepare it evidently were given in late 1968. Interestingly, Jackson's interest in the topic and his sense of its relevance antedated the Sino-Soviet border skirmishes.

8. U.S., Congress, Senate, Committee on Government Operations, Subcommittee on National Security and International Operations, *International Negotiation; When the Academic Door to Peking Opens.* Committee Print, 91st Cong., 2d sess., 1970.

9. Henry M. Jackson, "America in the World of the 70s," address to the Commonwealth Club of California, San Francisco, California, 5 March 1971. Jackson Papers, University of Washington Libraries, Seattle.

10. Henry M. Jackson, "A Perspective on American Foreign Policy," address to the World Affairs Council, Boston, Massachusetts, 22 April 1971. Jackson Papers, University of Washington Libraries, Seattle.

11. U.S., Congress, Senate, *China and American Policy,* Report of Senator Henry M. Jackson to the Committee on Armed Services. Committee Print, 93d Cong., 2d sess., 1974.

U.S., Congress, Senate, *China and United States Policy,* Report of Senator Henry M. Jackson to the Committee on Armed Services and the Committee on Energy and Natural Resources. Committee Print, Pub. No. 95–94, 95th Cong., 2d sess., 1978.

U.S., Congress, Senate, *China and the United States,* Report of Senator Henry M. Jackson to the Committee on Armed Services and the Committee on Energy and Natural Resources. Committee Print, Pub. No. 96–35, 96th Cong., 1st sess., 1979.

U.S., Congress, Senate, *The China Policy of Senator Henry M. Jackson,* Staff Report to the Committee on Armed Sevices. Committee Print, 98th Cong., 1st sess., 1983.

12. *China and United States Policy,* Committee Print, 1978, pp. 1–2.
13. *China and the United States,* Committee Print, 1979, p. 9.
14. Ibid., p. 10.

THE CENTRAL AMERICA COMMISSION

1. U.S., Congress, Senate, "Toward a Long-Term Policy for Central America," statement by Senator Jackson on the floor of the Senate, 98th Cong., 1st sess., 12 May 1983, *Congressional Record* 129:6553 (Daily Edition).
2. Ibid.
3. U.S., Congress, Senate, Committee on Government Operations, Subcommittee on National Policy Machinery, *Organizing for National Security, Vol. 3, Staff Reports and Recommendations,* Final Statement of Senator Henry M. Jackson, 87th Cong., 1st sess., 1961, p. 4.
4. Henry M. Jackson, "Labor and the U.S.-Central American Policy," address to Labor Law Conference honoring Edward Carlough, President, Sheet Metal Workers International Association, Hofstra School of Law, Hempstead, New York, 29 April 1983. Jackson Papers, University of Washington Libraries, Seattle.
5. Ibid.
6. U.S., The National Bipartisan Commission on Central America, Report, 10 January 1984.
7. Charles Krauthammer, "Whatever Became of the American Center?" In *Cutting Edges; Making Sense of the 80's* (New York: Random House, 1985), p. 98.

POSTSCRIPT

1. George F. Will, "The Finest Public Servant I Have Known" (September 6, 1983). In *The Morning After; American Successes and Excesses 1981–1986* (New York: The Free Press, 1986), p. 409.